INSIDE LOOKING UP

Inspiring Innovative Escalation in Healthcare Risk & Safety Ecosystems

Editors:
Jeffrey F. Driver, JD, MBA
Renée Bernard, JD
Lorri Zipperer, MA

THE RISK **AUTHORITY**

STANFORD

ISBN-13: 978-0-9971226-0-2
ISBN-13: 978-0-9971226-1-9 (pbk)

Script excerpts from *Field of Dreams*, Universal Studios, 1989, used with permission.
Printed in USA: John S. Swift Co., Inc.

The Risk Authority Stanford
PO Box 60790, Palo Alto, CA 94306
T 650 723 6824   F 650 736 2495
info@theriskauthority.com
theriskauthority.com

TWILIGHT IS THE TIME FOR DREAMS;
DAYLIGHT THE TIME FOR ACTION.

WE DEDICATE THIS BOOK
TO THE COMING OF A NEW DAWN,
AND TO THE PROMISE OF RISK AND
PATIENT SAFETY MANAGEMENT.

TABLE OF CONTENTS

FOREWORD

A HOT AND SULTRY SUMMER NIGHT in the dog days of August, I was working the night shift as a float orderly in an urban community hospital. It was a shift that started like any other; but this one was different. This was a night that would dramatically change lives—including mine.

Let's call him Jimmy, a child somewhere between eight and ten years old who lived in this aging blue-collar Midwest neighborhood. His mom brought him to the emergency room because his breathing had changed and she was worried. The emergency physician diagnosed Jimmy's loud wheezing as a bad case of croup. At this time, some thirty years ago, he would have been treated and released.

This night, however, Jimmy was admitted to the hospital and sent to 2 South; known to me as the Stroke Floor where the majority of patients were elderly with a variety of medical needs including extended rehabilitation from cerebrovascular accidents, or CVAs.

I transferred Jimmy from the emergency room gurney to his bed. The nursing supervisor had reassigned me from the emergency department to 2 South as things were busy on the floor, so I got to follow Jimmy. Within minutes of arrival, Jimmy's breathing worsened. The house physician was paged but while he was in transit, Jimmy's high-pitched gasps turned silent. While Jimmy struggled to find even a wisp of air, he turned from pale grey to blue and the panic in his eyes dimmed as he fell into unconsciousness. Jimmy's struggle to breathe ceased. The clinical team snapped into action.

The overhead page blared "Code blue 2 South, Code blue 2 South, Code blue 2 South." The team rushed to the bedside with the code cart, but now the panic was ours. The nurse scrambled for the laryngoscope and endotracheal tube that would be Jimmy's lifeline, but despite her frantic search there was no pediatric equipment in the cart. Someone was asked to run to the surgical floor for the equipment, but it was too late, Jimmy's heart stopped beating. Despite numerous attempts, an airway could not be secured. Forced positive pressure leaked outside the bag and mask as the respiratory therapist labored to deliver lifesaving air and oxygen, filling the room with an unsettling honking noise I had never heard before.

It seemed to last forever. But after ten or fifteen minutes passed, the code was called. Jimmy was pronounced dead.

I don't remember much from there. I remember crying by myself in a completely dark, empty waiting room abandoned in the still of the night. I remember the medical team crying as well and not being able to look each other in the eye. The family came and joined Jimmy's mom. A priest came. They left. Somehow the clinical team carried on that night.

I remember the next evening when I crawled back to work. I was asked not to speak about the prior evening, what had happened, what hadn't happened. Rumor thrived in this silent space. I heard that the parents were told that Jimmy had died of natural causes due to a serious condition called epiglottitis and that he could not be saved. No mention of the problems I had witnessed. I never heard anything more and as I was told, I said nothing more. Soon talk of that night faded away. Yet, over the coming weeks and months, then years—I promised myself I would do whatever I could to make sure this could never happen again.

I became a pediatric respiratory therapist working in one of the nation's best pediatric hospitals. Yet, all of my training did not prepare me for what then was not addressed in clinical training: medical error—its causes, its scope, its prevention. Its crushing impact on patients, families, and providers. I became a patient representative and then a risk manager, only to witness an endless repeating pattern of lives lost to preventable medical error that should not have been.

This isn't to say some progress hasn't been made in the last thirty years in keeping patients safe as they move through medical systems. Individuals and institutions around the world have devoted themselves to changing healthcare for the better, and as a result, we have made some miraculous strides in our medicines, our technologies, and our practices. But our progress to date towards keeping patients safe from medical harm falls woefully short of perfection, or even really, good enough. To say otherwise is an injustice; too many lives are slipping away due to preventable medical error.

A 2013 review from the *Journal of Patient Safety* estimates that in the United States alone, between 210,000 and 400,000 patients each year that go to the hospital for care suffer some type of preventable harm that contributes to their death.[1] This means that even if we were to take the lower threshold of this estimate, 575 lives will be lost unnecessarily today, tomorrow, and every day— every year. Now more than ever, clinical enterprise risk management and patient safety systems must bear the burden of that number; they must become more effective and efficient; they must seek out solutions to fully and finally eradicate medical error. Zero harm must not just be aspirational words, but the central, unequivocal, and measurable focus of risk management and patient safety work.

Some years before this study, Douglas Hubbard published his 2009 book, *The Failure of Risk Management: Why It's Broken and How to Fix It*, in which he asserts that the prevailing methods of managing risk across all industries are not doing what they set out to do.[2] Industry executives are not paying enough attention to the outcomes of their strategies; they are failing to measure whether or not their methods are successful. In today's healthcare context, this results in 575 people dying who shouldn't have.

Hubbard was right: managers of risk and safety, ourselves among them, were not and are not focused enough on measuring the effectiveness of our strategies. Inspired by Hubbard's call to action, the risk management team at The Risk Authority Stanford set out on a new path to rethink everything we were doing. We set out to strengthen our risk analysis methods and enhance our management processes. More than this, we were inspired to develop our own evidence-based methodologies for managing risk and keeping patients at the center of our vision. Toward this end we launched Innovence™, a platform dedicated to the art and science of risk management effectiveness, and we made a commitment to focus on evidence and innovation equally with the patient at the center of our focus.

It is not enough to favor one over the other. Evidence without a defined process to escalate innovation will never move the mountains of factors driving medical error that so urgently need moving; innovation ultimately requires evidence to sustain momentum—though we mustn't stall progress by relying solely on evidence as a catalyst to ignite the process. But there is no simple answer, and there is no one right way to approach this challenge. Rather, there are infinite possibilities for how to take action and transform the way risk and safety are managed in healthcare; our approach is simply one possibility.

As managers of risk we should be unsettled by our lack of effectiveness, and work to seriously step-up innovation with the end point of moving from 575 to zero harm in a demonstrable way. But rather than debating or dwelling on how risk methods have failed in the past, it is vital to pick ourselves up and pursue a new course of action, to see the hope and inspiration that comes with innovation and advancement, to shine light into dark places and bring them to light.

To change risk management, what are you willing to risk?

Risk management has the potential to transform the safety of healthcare; to generate actionable risk intelligence; to enable faster adaptation of targeted solutions; to mitigate loss and create value; to reduce harm and improve patient safety. The practice of risk management is rich with untapped potential, and as we mine its depths, the promise of risk management will burst to the surface— the commitment to support and protect patients and clinicians, and to offer care that doesn't falter.

Now more than ever, it is a time for reflection and revelation; a time to reevaluate and seek answers; a time to prepare and take action. Healthcare risk management is on the brink of a new frontier. It's time to break through the barriers that have long hampered our progress in eradicating medical error by modernizing preconceived ideas, building on traditional working approaches, and embracing the new. It's time to look at things through a new lens, with new clarity, and new focus. It's time to drive ourselves to be creative thinkers, to push the limit of what's possible, to become innovators.

The biggest risk you'll ever take is not taking the risk to innovate.

But where do we start? The world around us is evolving, and sweeping reform in healthcare, economics, and politics can create seemingly insurmountable challenges. The idea of change can be daunting when we aren't sure where it might bring us, or how far we must travel along its winding road. But changes must be made; lives depend on it.

So we start by rethinking our positions and our priorities, reexamining our values and processes, and then reorganizing ourselves, teams, and structures. At The Risk Authority Stanford we know that the future of healthcare risk management brims with the possibility to change lives, and we are committed to doing everything in our power to help make that change happen. We are, quite literally, inside, looking up.

This book is not a guide or a checklist (though our next book will be more along these lines). Rather, it's a beginning. It is a turning of the key in order to unlock the door for changes to be made. It's our attempt to create a channel for discovery that opens minds to innovation and helps to carve space for creation.

It is my fervent hope that you will reach for this information-rich book over and over, and that *Inside Looking Up* will help to inspire new and innovative approaches to managing risk and patient safety holistically and strategically. I hope that at this twilight in healthcare, readers will use this book as a treasure trove of new ideas, and that the book will inspire you to continue mining the depths of its pages, always discovering something new. Ultimately, it's my hope that it will spark new ideas and conversations, and that together we will redouble and escalate efforts to innovate, collect, and follow evidence that can make a difference on a significant scale.

There is no destination but the journey. There is no end point but continual improvement and perpetual renewal of our unending promise to try, perhaps to fail in the attempt, but then to try harder until we succeed—and then to do it again.

Thirty years have passed since Jimmy's life was lost; thirty years since I first made that promise to myself. And how many countless lives have been lost since? It's time for us all to renew the promises we've made to ourselves and our patients. It's time to reawaken. It's time to wrap the tenets of these pages around ourselves like armor and charge into the fray. It's time to question everything, to think bigger and faster, to motivate each other, to build upon what we have to make our futures stronger and brighter. It's time to reenergize our battle with a faceless enemy and refuse to surrender.

It's time to lead the charge.

Jeffrey F. Driver
Chief Executive Officer
The Risk Authority Stanford, LLC
Stanford, California USA

References
1. James JT. A new evidence-based estimate of patient harms associated with hospital care. *J Patient Saf.* 2013;9(3):122-128.

2. Hubbard DW. *The Failure of Risk Management: Why It's Broken and How to Fix It.* Hoboken, NJ: Wiley; 2009.

ABOUT THIS BOOK

***INSIDE LOOKING UP* CHAMPIONS INNOVATION** as the catalyst to transforming the healthcare industry—and risk management in particular—into a proactive, predictive, and dynamic force. Through the voices of the team at The Risk Authority Stanford and other experts in the industry, this book explores the role of innovators in risk and safety management strategies and how they can: reenergize health systems, generate actionable risk intelligence, enable responsive adaptation to targeted solutions, mitigate loss, and create value. Ultimately, innovators can help to usher in a new era of risk and safety management that keeps patients at the forefront of its vision while reducing harm, improving engagement, and saving lives.

By comparing the landscape of healthcare to the inspirational film *Field of Dreams*, *Inside Looking Up* discusses ways to innovate in the healthcare space, why it matters, and offers a powerful example of how listening to and acting on the call for change can achieve greater heights of success than ever imagined. Ultimately, *Field of Dreams* is used to demonstrate the power of disruptive innovation by exploring how a community, led by an inspired innovator, embarks on a journey of change.

So it's time to grab some popcorn, fire up your media viewer of choice, and pop in *Field of Dreams*. This classic story will facilitate a deeper understanding of its application as a metaphor. Between sips of soda, take note of how Ray Kinsella charts a new course of action as he responds to a voice that whispers,

"If You Build It, He Will Come." The power of this idea translates seamlessly to the healthcare space. As Ray makes the determination that trying is worth the risk, and thus plows down his corn crop to build a baseball diamond, so too must those in the healthcare space. The determination must be made that risks are necessary for growth and transformation. In particular, managers of risk must be willing to reorganize, redesign, and readjust in order to build a new field for patients, clinicians, and organizations. As applied to healthcare, *Field of Dreams* offers a glimpse of what this process can look like, how success can be achieved and why seeking out and committing to new practices can forever change the playing field.

Inside Looking Up is divided into four parts—drawn from the messages moving inspiration forward in the film:

- **PART I: IF YOU BUILD IT, HE WILL COME: MOTIVATION TO LEAD AND DRIVE CHANGE**
  Part I establishes innovation as both a choice and a commitment, and encourages leaders to step up to the plate. It sets the stage for innovators to assess and explore their own and other's level of engagement in the process of innovation. Part I also provides an overview of the history and evolution of the risk management profession.

- **PART II: EASE HIS PAIN: INNOVATION IN HEALTHCARE RISK MANAGEMENT**
  Part II discusses the importance of building and maintaining relationships by meeting both personal and professional needs. It offers insight on the importance of collaborating with valuable stakeholders, from patients to clinicians, and provides examples of how disruptive innovative can create value.

- **PART III: GO THE DISTANCE: COMMITMENT TO THE DREAM OF CHANGE**
  Part III focuses on the role of traditional risk management practices and the evolving needs of stakeholders. It prepares managers of risk to reassess hiring practices, to reexamine the effectiveness of traditional risk methods, and to approach problem solving from a different direction. To this end, three vignettes are provided to demonstrate how holistic understanding and innovative hacking can save and transform lives and practices.

- **PART IV: BUILD IT AND THEY WILL COME: STRUCTURE AND STRATEGY FOR LASTING CHANGE**

  Part IV discusses creating spaces and structures for innovative practices to endure. It offers useful tools for healthcare risk managers to enhance risk mitigation strategies, such as the incorporation of design thinking, decision quality, and decision analysis. Lastly, it prepares innovators to encourage and obtain collaboration for their vision, and to sustain the dream.

What this Book is Not

Inside Looking Up isn't meant to serve as a standard "how to" – that was not its goal. It instead aims to help readers see a new way, to approach the well-worn path of risk management differently. It is meant to spark advocates for change, to inspire partners for improvement, and to motivate new conversations. It is not a checklist. Rather, it is a beginning.

Who Should Read this Book

While there are many people that agree things should be done differently in the healthcare industry, not all of them are willing to take the actions necessary for transformation. This book is intended for those who are activated for change; for those who believe things can and should be done differently to make patients safe and practices better, and are ready and willing to take action. Certainly not everyone can be a great visionary, but everyone can contribute to a better vision. It's worth taking the time to consider the impact that a genuine commitment to transformation can have, how it can improve risk strategies, create value, and keep patients, employees and organizations healthy and safe.

Inside Looking Up begins the conversation on these topics, focusing specifically on the role of innovators within the context of managing risk in healthcare. It asks, among other questions:

- How can we approach innovation with energy, while also remaining thoughtful and careful?
- Is there a way to integrate creative solutions with evidence-based methodologies?
- How can innovation make risk managing strategies stronger and more reliable?
- How can tradition and innovative risk methods inform and enhance each other?

- What can we draw from the expertise of others to motivate acceptance of change?

This book is for those who share these questions and a commitment to discovering, as much as it is possible, the answers to them. It is for change agents or agents of change. It is for leaders who recognize the need to change the way they manage risk, as well as for managers of risk who "hear the voice" and are in search of tools to motivate others to action.

How to Read this Book

- Why the prologue?: The prologue sets the course for the narrative journey. It provides necessary terminologies about types of innovators, and clarifies the use of metaphor. Though some may be inclined to breeze past prologues in their eagerness to get at the heart of a text, it's important that readers give the prologue of *Inside Looking Up* their undivided attention in order to fully understand and appreciate the application of *Field of Dreams* to the practice of risk and safety management. In addition, Appendix One provides a quick plot synopsis to help readers track primary developments to weave the story together as appropriate for this text.

- Icons: Visual cues are provided to help guide readers through the application of the metaphor of *Field of Dreams* to the healthcare industry. The icons serve as signals to organize topics and draw reader attention to different aspects of the metaphor.

- Your voice: Each chapter offers a space labeled "YOUR VOICE." This space is envisioned as a place for readers to take notes or sketch ideas. It's a space for readers to apply the chapter's concepts to their own experience, to brainstorm, to question, and to explore.

- Inspirational readings: Each chapter ends with additional readings to inform and inspire further thinking and action for change.

- Building your own field: *Field of Dreams* ends in a hopeful twilight in which anything seems possible. We wanted to conclude with a similar feeling, and provide readers with a space for possibility. After the final chapter, we've created this space for you to begin to conceptualize your own field of dreams.

ABOUT THE CONTRIBUTORS

CRAIG ALBANESE is vice president of quality and performance improvement at Lucile Packard Children's Hospital Stanford. In this role, he is responsible for overseeing the organization's lean and quality transformation. Craig is also a pediatric general surgeon, professor of surgery, and holds the John A. and Cynthia Fry Gunn Directorship of Surgical Services. Albanese earned his undergraduate degree in natural sciences and mathematics from Washington and Lee University. He earned his medical degree at Downstate Medical Center, subsequently completing his general surgery training at The Mount Sinai Hospital in New York and his pediatric surgery fellowship at the Children's Hospital of Pittsburgh. He was on the faculty at the University of Pittsburgh followed by the University of California, San Francisco before joining the faculty at Stanford in 2002. In 2008 he earned a MBA from Santa Clara University's Leavey School of Business.

ANDREW AZAN, is the Vice President of Business Development at The Risk Authority Stanford. Andrew has dedicated over 18 years of his career working with hospitals and health systems in providing patient safety and risk mitigation solutions. Andrew's passion for patient safety and solving complex problems within healthcare has been widely recognized and earned him the honor of serving on the boards for the American Association of Safe Patient Handling Professionals (2011) and the University of Texas Arlington—Nursing School Smart Hospital (2008). Andrew's passion for healthcare stems from his family who has a long history as providers and his son who at an early age was diagnosed with a heart condition. Having the good fortune of understanding "how the system works," Andrew was able to help his son get the treatment he needed to live a normal life. This experience was what inspired Andrew to commit his career to making healthcare better and safer for everyone

RENÉE BERNARD is a healthcare risk management professional specializing in developing and applying evidence-based risk management safety solutions. She serves as Vice President of Clinical Risk and Safety at The Risk Authority Stanford. In her role, she works collaboratively with hospital, medical and physician leadership through the full cycle of the risk management process, including the identification and assessment of risk, the evaluation of potential solutions, the selection of strategy and mitigation projects, and monitoring progress to goals. Renée received her JD degree from Santa Clara University School of Law with certification in Health Law and received her BA in English and Linguistics from California State University East Bay.

GRAHAM BILLINGHAM is the Chief Medical Officer, Medical Protective Company (MedPro). Dr. Billingham attended Stanford University as an undergraduate in Biology, medical school at UCLA Medical Center and completed his residency in Emergency Medicine at Harbor-UCLA Medical Center. He is board certified and is a Fellow of the American College of Emergency Physicians and the American Academy of Emergency Medicine. Dr. Billingham has 26 years of experience as an emergency medicine physician. He speaks nationally on emergency medicine and has lectured in more than 250 CME courses on risk management, operations, documentation, patient safety, information technology, coding and billing, and malpractice prevention. As Chief Medical Officer, he is responsible for leading MedPro Group's Healthcare Advisory Boards and working with the Business Council to support clinical risk, claims, underwriting and sales efforts. Most recently Dr. Billingham served as President & CEO for Emergency Physicians Insurance Company Risk Retention Group. He has also served on the physician advisory boards of several technology and insurance companies, the American College of Emergency Physicians Medical Legal Committee and

Coding and Nomenclature Committee. He is Emeritus Chairman of the Emergency Medicine Patient Safety Foundation and has served on the Board of Emergency Department Practice Management Association. He founded and served as Medical Director for The Center for Emergency Medical Education and was a co-founder of the National Emergency Medicine Board Review Course.

JAMES CONWAY is an adjunct lecturer at the Harvard School of Public Health in Boston. From 2006-2009 he was Senior Vice President of the Institute for Healthcare Improvement (IHI) and from 2005-2011, Senior Fellow. During 1995-2005, he was Executive Vice President and Chief Operating Officer of Dana-Farber Cancer Institute (DFCI), Boston. Prior to joining DFCI, he had a 27-year career at Children's Hospital, Boston in radiology administration, finance, and as Assistant Hospital Director. His areas of expertise and interest include governance and executive leadership, patient safety, change management, crisis management, and patient-/ family-centered care. He holds a MS from Lesley College, Cambridge, Massachusetts. Jim is the winner of numerous awards including the 1999 American College of Healthcare Executives/Massachusetts Regents Award, the 2001 first Individual Leadership Award in Patient Safety by the Joint Commission on Accreditation of Healthcare Organizations and the National Committee for Quality Assurance. In 2008, he received the Picker Award for Excellence in the Advancement of Patient Centered Care, in 2009 the Mary Davis Barber Heart of Hospice Award from the Massachusetts Hospice and Palliative Care Federation, and in 2012 both the Institute for Patient and Family Centered Care Leadership Award and the first Honorary Fellowship of the National Association for Healthcare Quality. A Lifetime Fellow of the American College of Healthcare Executives, he has served as a Distinguished Advisor to the Lucian Leape Institute for the National Patient Safety Foundation. Institute of Medicine Committee service has included Identifying and Preventing Medication Errors, a Learning Healthcare System, and Optimizing Access and Scheduling. Current Board service includes: board member, Winchester Hospital/Lahey Health; board member & chair of the Quality of Care Committee, Lahey Health System; board member & vice-chair, American Cancer Society, New England Region; and member, Board of Visitors, University of Massachusetts, Boston.

JEFFREY DRIVER has more than 25 years of experience as a risk management professional and has managed the enterprise risk in community, tertiary, and academic medical centers. Jeff currently serves as the Chief Executive Officer of The Risk Authority Stanford, and as the Chief Risk Officer of Stanford Health Care and Stanford Children's Health. Before joining Stanford, he was Chief Risk Officer and Director of Regulatory Advocacy at the Beth Israel Deaconess Medical Center in Boston. Jeff is a member of the State Bar of California and has been designated as a Distinguished Fellow by the American Society for Healthcare Risk Management (ASHRM) and as an Associate in Risk Management by the Insurance Institute of America. In 2008, he was awarded membership to the Risk Management Honor Roll by *Business Insurance* magazine. He is a past president of ASHRM (2004), served on its board of directors, and was steering committee chair of its JCAHO Liaison, Advocacy and Legislative & Regulatory Affairs task forces. Jeff is also a CRM (Certified Risk Manager) National Faculty Member for The National Alliance for Insurance Education & Research, and has also served as faculty to ASHRM's Barton Certificate in Healthcare Risk Management Program and to the Harvard Medical School. Jeff earned a JD from Thomas Jefferson School of Law in San Diego, an MBA from Cleveland State University, a BS in Allied Health Clinical Professions from Ohio State University, and is an American Hospital Association/National Patient Safety Foundation Patient Safety Leadership Fellow. Jeff is starting his next academic journey to earn a PhD which, subject to admission, follows on from the MSc program at University of Oxford in which he is currently enrolled. His thesis prospectus is to study and pinpoint the evidence of risk management system effectiveness in a diversity of healthcare settings across the United Kingdom and the United States of America.

ED HALL currently serves as the Chief Operating Officer of The Risk Authority Stanford. In his current role at The Risk Authority Stanford, Ed oversees clinical risk management, workplace solutions and claims and litigation operations. With over 20 years of diverse risk and insurance management experience, Ed is an authority in managing risks in healthcare and industrial sectors. He is nationally recognized for his development of innovative loss control risk management programs, which have led to dramatic increases in both patient safety and financial savings. Additionally, his knowledge and leadership helped Stanford Hospital and Clinics receive the Best Practice Award for safe patient handling—one of The Risk

Authority Stanford's key strategic patient and employee initiatives. Ed received a BS in Fire and Safety Engineering and a MS in Loss Prevention and Safety from Eastern Kentucky University and is also a Certified Safety Professional. Ed also received a certificate in Strategic Decision and Risk Management from Stanford University's Center for Professional Development.

MARY ANNE HILLIARD is Executive Vice President and Chief Legal Officer of Children's National Health System, in Washington DC. She oversees Legal Services, Risk Management, Compliance, Internal Audit, Insurance, Workers Compensation, and Captive Management. In addition to being a lawyer, Mary Anne is a registered nurse who practiced at Children's National in the early part of her career. She went on to practice law in Washington, DC, specializing in healthcare law issues and malpractice defense. She is extensively published and lectures widely at hospitals, universities and associations on health law issues. Committed to the concept that the best way to manage risk is to prevent it, she has led many local and national grant funded initiatives to share risk data and study pediatric outcomes to reduce serious adverse events. On the financial side of risk management, she was involved in the creation of two captive insurance companies and is responsible for the ongoing operation of those corporate entities. Under her leadership, her organization has enjoyed numerous patient safety awards and distinctions including Leapfrog Designation six years in a row; the Child Health Corporation of America Race for Results award (two times), the George Mason Quality Improvement of the Year Award, and the DC Hospital Association Patient Safety Award. After serving many years as her local American Society of Healthcare Risk Management (ASHRM) chapter president, she was elected to serve a three-year term on the National Board of ASHRM for whom she served as the Society's president in 2012.

JOHN LITTIG is the Chief Finance and Underwriting Officer of The Risk Authority Stanford. John began his career with Aon working in the Healthcare Practice Group providing alternative risk consulting for healthcare providers around the US. John was honored as an Aon Excellence Roundtable Attendee in 2010. John was the co-author and co-creator of *Aon's Healthcare Captive Benchmark Study*. Now at The Risk Authority Stanford, John's passion is working to apply modern data techniques including natural language processing and machine learning to accelerate the risk management cycle in healthcare. John works to connect traditional approaches to risk information actuarial analysis with decision analysis tools to form a complete understanding of total value of risk. Through these efforts, John enables the use of risk finance as a tool to drive desired risk behaviors throughout the Stanford Health Care enterprise. Recently John has been a speaker at several healthcare captive conferences including Captive Insurance Company Association, Bermuda Captive Conference and Hawaii Captive Insurance Council. John is currently pursuing his JD at Santa Clara University School of Law. John holds a BA from Miami University and is recognized as Associate in Risk Management by the Insurance Institute of America.

SIMON MAWER is Assistant Vice President of Risk Strategy and Design at The Risk Authority Stanford, where he leverages his unique experience in law, decision science and design thinking to assist clients in applying leading approaches to solve systemic healthcare challenges. As part of the Innovence Lab™ at The Risk Authority Stanford, Simon leads interdisciplinary teams from across the Stanford ecosystem and beyond in using design thinking to generate solutions that improve patient safety and clinical outcomes. As a lead facilitator, Simon also consults with client executives and legal teams in using decision science tools to make high-quality capital investment and litigation strategy decisions. Prior to joining the team, Simon practiced as a commercial and personal injury lawyer in Australia. He received his law degree from the University of Technology, Sydney, is admitted as a lawyer to the Supreme Court of New South Wales, and holds a Certificate in Strategic Decisions and Risk Management from Stanford University.

RYAN MEADE is the Director of Regulatory Compliance Studies at Loyola University Chicago School of Law. He teaches courses addressing both long-standing and emerging regulatory challenges for healthcare organizations and oversees Loyola's regulatory compliance curriculum. Ryan also practices law with Meade, Roach & Annulis, LLP and is a managing director of Aegis Compliance & Ethics Center, LLP. For over nearly 25 years, his legal and consulting practice has focused on advising organizations on compliance programs and the strategies for managing regulatory risk. Mr. Meade received his undergraduate degree from Northwestern University and his JD from Cornell University.

GISELE NORRIS has for the past 20 years provided strategic consulting and risk advice to large, complex healthcare accounts. Her career began in Latin America, where she worked to build a new culture of healthcare risk finance and management. As insurance capacity became scarce during the hard market of 2001, Gisele shifted her focus to assisting large American healthcare entities to build and leverage sophisticated and responsive alternative risk vehicles, such as captives and risk retention groups. Today, she leads Aon's healthcare practice in the western United States. In this capacity, she assists clients and colleagues to provide innovative solutions to healthcare entities and also directly provides strategic consulting services to select institutions. Gisele received her BA from the University of California at Berkeley in 1988; MPH and MPA degrees from Columbia University in 1994; and a DrPH (with specialties in epidemiology and health policy) from the University of California at Berkeley in 2000. Gisele is fluent in Spanish and proficient in French.

DANA ORQUIZA is a healthcare risk management professional whose experience includes working as a medical-surgical nurse and an associate attorney at medical malpractice defense firms in Washington, DC. She is the Assistant Vice President of Clinical Risk and Safety at The Risk Authority Stanford. In her role, Dana provides risk management consultations and education to staff and healthcare providers at Stanford Health Care and Stanford Children's Health. Her combination of clinical and legal expertise is instrumental in effectively managing risk proactively through value creation and value protection. Dana received her BSN from Georgetown University and her JD from the Catholic University of America.

KIM PARDINI-KIELY serves as Vice President for Safety & Risk Strategic Ventures for The Risk Authority Stanford. She is a healthcare executive experienced in leading hospital operations and in driving clinical improvements in outcomes. She is a nationally recognized expert in improving clinical outcomes, implementing clinical analytic departments, transforming hospital culture and creating models that focus on value. Her convictions are that compassionate and respectful care must be delivered across the continuum and out within the community so that partnerships can support the health and well-being of patients and their families. Kim has been recognized for her contributions to diversity in receiving the first ever Excellence for Healthcare Diversity award.

LEILANI SCHWEITZER did not choose a career in healthcare, it chose her. In 2005, her son, Gabriel, died after a series of medical mistakes. As Assistant Vice President for Communication and Resolution at The Risk Authority Stanford, she works in risk management at the same hospital where those errors happened. In her work Leilani uses her own experience with medical errors to navigate between the often insular, legal and administrative sides of medical error; and the intricate, emotional side of the patient and family experience. Her work with The Risk Authority Stanford gives her a unique view of the importance and complex realities of disclosure and transparency in healthcare. Leilani speaks nationally and internationally about her work on communication and resolution after unexpected medical events.

MANUEL SOLIS has been involved in the claims arena since 1981, as a claim adjuster, supervisor and consultant. He currently serves as Assistant Vice President of Worker's Compensation Claims Administration at The Risk Authority Stanford. His emphasis is to ensure the timely and appropriate delivery of benefits to employees and reduction of claims management costs.

JOHN VAUGHAN is a safety professional with 35 years of experience in the areas of Industrial Safety, Industrial Hygiene, and Ergonomics. He was Senior Safety Engineer with The Risk Authority Stanford, is a Certified Professional Ergonomist, and manages the ergonomics programs at Stanford Health Care and Stanford Children's Health. John's professional experience includes work in the insurance industry, electronics and semi-conductor manufacturing, ergonomics consulting services, and healthcare. He has published articles in the American Association of Occupational Health Nurses, *Advances in Human Aspects of Healthcare*—a publication comprised of presentations at the 2014 Applied Human Factors and Ergonomics Conference, and white papers on safe patient handling, safety professionals' staffing levels in healthcare, as well as a blog on loss control and prevention issues in risk management. John holds a MSc in Engineering and has been associated with Stanford University Medical Center for 10 years.

DANA WELLE began her professional life as a busy obstetrician-gynecologist after completing her residency in a large tertiary academic medical center. She has more than 16 years of clinical experience and managed high risk obstetrical cases and performed complicated gynecological surgery while in private practice. Her focus has always been on the care and safety of her patients. She is a fellow in the American College of Obstetrics and Gynecology and also a fellow in the American College of Surgeons. Although she is no longer directly involved in patient care, she continues her pursuit of medical knowledge to improve her understanding of potential risks physicians and care providers face on a daily basis. While practicing medicine, Dana attended law school with an emphasis in health law, and is a member of the State Bar Association of California. Moving into risk management was a natural transition for Dana with both of her advanced degrees and she currently serves as the Chief Medical Executive of The Risk Authority Stanford. She is also the co-chairman of the Stanford Committee for Professional Satisfaction and Support, previously the Wellness Committee, and the Director of the Peer Support Program. Her focus on provider wellness and professional fulfillment are a unique view into the importance of considering provider health's impact on patient safety and risk management. Dana received her BS in Kinesiology from the University of California at Los Angeles, her DO degree from the Western University of Health Sciences, and her JD degree from Santa Clara University School of Law.

MATTHEW WOLDEN is executive director for the Center for Quality & Clinical Effectiveness at Stanford Children's Health and Lucile Packard Children's Hospital Stanford. In this capacity, Matthew is responsible for overseeing the divisions of quality improvement, patient safety, infection prevention and control, analytics and clinical effectiveness, accreditation and regulatory compliance, professional practice evaluation, research and innovation, and trauma. Prior to joining Stanford, Matthew was the administrator for the women's health service line at New York-Presbyterian, the University Hospital of Columbia and Cornell. Matthew completed his undergraduate and graduate training in public health at the University of Nevada, Reno.

ELAINE ZIEMBA serves as Vice President, Risk Consulting for The Risk Authority Stanford. From the start of her career, Elaine has focused on the empathetic, patient-centered elements of risk management strategies and outcomes. Elaine has developed effective risk management programs in a variety of settings, inclusive of academic medical centers, integrated delivery systems, multi-hospital community based systems, insurance and insurance services organizations and now her expertise is shared on a consulting basis. Recognized for her ability to blend the theory with evidenced-based practice and practical considerations, Elaine lives by the guideline that in an uncertain and often complicated world, keeping the patient at the focal point will support determination of the right approach for all involved. Elaine adheres to the practice that good patient safety and good risk management strategies should be shared for the betterment of patients and families, healthcare organizations and the risk management profession. As such, she is recognized as a leader and mentor and continues to be an active member of various healthcare and risk management professional associations. Elaine has her undergraduate degree from the University of Maryland, her MHA from The George Washington University and her JD from Golden Gate University.

LORRI ZIPPERER, Cybrarian is the principal at Zipperer Project Management in Albuquerque, NM. Lorri was a founding staff member of the US-based National Patient Safety Foundation where she launched the first listserv and evidence-update service on patient safety. Through her work and teaching she focuses on a systems-safety orientation to evidence, information and knowledge (EIK) access and use. Lorri works to bring together multidisciplinary teams to envision, design and implement EIK initiatives. In addition, she has been the development editor for the US government-funded AHRQ Patient Safety Network since its inception. Lorri is honored to be the only member of her profession to participate in the American Hospital Association/National Patient Safety Foundation Patient Safety Leadership Fellowship program. She was recognized with an Institute for Safe Medication Practices Cheers award for her work with librarians, libraries and their involvement in patient safety. In addition to her role in *Inside Looking Up*, Ms Zipperer has developed several other publications on patient safety including two 2014 texts for Gower Publications, UK on knowledge management and evidence, information, and knowledge transfer in patient safety.

THE RISK AUTHORITY STANFORD

THE GOAL OF THE RISK AUTHORITY STANFORD, first and foremost, is to help save lives and prevent harm to patients. We believe risk management can and should be used to foster sustainable improvements in patient outcomes and satisfaction, as well as in risk financing and hospital performance. We are committed to creating a safer, more responsive healthcare landscape through personal involvement, cutting-edge technologies, superior analysis and award-winning solutions that are both affordable and accessible.

Over the last twenty years, our team at The Risk Authority Stanford has had the honor of collaborating with members of the Stanford University Medical Network of hospitals and healthcare organizations as we provide them with our risk management services. We've gained invaluable knowledge and insight by engaging with and learning from leadership and frontline staff, physicians, care workers, and the many bright and curious minds at Stanford. We've been fortunate to absorb and learn from their passion, commitment, and perseverance —and we've dedicated ourselves to reflecting these values in the practices, expertise, and solutions we now offer to Stanford and beyond, as we strive to effect change in how risk management is practiced around the world.

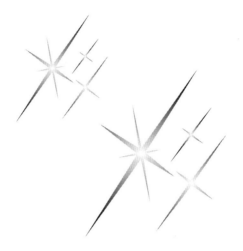

ACKNOWLEDGEMENTS:

Over the course of the development of *Inside Looking Up*, we drew from a varied and impressive set of colleagues and friends during the time we went from concept to hard copy. Time, commitment and interest benefit the editors in ways that are worth recognizing in print.

We would first like to recognize the experts that helped us see the value in the endeavor. Geri Amori, Michelle Oberman, Pravene Nath, Carlos Cruz, Ann McCune, Donna Thomas and chapter authors James Conway and Matthew Wolden shared their time and valuable insight with us as we formalized the concept. As the content began to take shape Lexie Darch, P. Divya Parikh, Carole Kulik, and Cheryl DeKleine volunteered their time in reading and commentary to further shape the language of the text. Joann Wleklinski brought detail and clarity to the writing while Jeannine Gluck indexed the material for the reader's ease of use.

The production team included a variety of individuals who brought polish to the final product. Karen Dangremond's thoughtful and fresh eye brought distinct design to the pages of the text; Nicole Fowler created a cover and corresponding web site that popped.

The Risk Authority Stanford team authored and coordinated chapters amidst their daily managing of risk and daily operations throughout the development process. This is a true testament to the dedication and professionalism of each employee. Finally—the amount of time and effort that is represented in these pages spilt into time at home as well. As with any project of this size and this duration, the editors drew from families and friends for support. Ross Vagnieres patiently listened to the stories of the development of text, made dinner, did laundry, and shuttled us from restaurants and airports to allow the editors to get the work done. Kahlil Dumas and Rosi Bernard provided valuable inspiration and motivation throughout this meaningful work. A special thank you to Kristin Driver for her editing insights and all of her guidance that helped to make this book shine.

This text was a growth experience for the editors, The Risk Authority Stanford as an organization, and we hope, will serve as one for healthcare risk management. We appreciate those who helped us make it happen.

**YOU SEE THINGS; AND YOU SAY
"WHY?" BUT I DREAM THINGS
THAT NEVER WERE; AND I SAY
"WHY NOT?"**

– George Bernard Shaw, *Back to Methuselah*

SEEING THE FIELD ANEW THROUGH METAPHOR

Ryan Meade, Jeffrey Driver, Lorri Zipperer

AS THE SUN SETS: INNOVATION BEGINS

There is something magical about the sky at sunset, as daylight dissipates. Skyscrapers begin to pop to life from the inside, their lit windows creating patterns across the darkening urban sky. Mountains in the southwest turn watermelon pink. Wheat in the Great Plains whispers soft good nights as their stalks shift from green to shadow. The evening calm opens the door to reflection—seeing and hearing the environment differently as the day enters a new phase to prepare for and consider tomorrow. For some people, the coming of evening is a time of regret; for others, it is a time to embrace a vision for the future: a time to hear a voice.

It could be said that the healthcare industry in general, and management of its risk in particular, are in this twilight, positioned at a moment of reflection—or should be. The reasons people enter the health professions are challenged by economic, personal, care, and technological complexities that are not anticipated by practitioners when they start out.[1-5] Stubborn troubles with resources, system design, and personal commitment all continue to weigh on healthcare professionals. Work to reduce medical error continues in earnest, evidenced by substantial activity and expense being applied with some shining stars and impressive results emerging,[6] yet few universal improvements are being achieved and sustained.[7,8] Indeed, something as fundamental as hand hygiene is still not controlled.[9] Costs continue to escalate, and steady streams of regulations seem poised to overwhelm budgets and schedules.[1,10] It's understandable why some see this as a bleak time with the sun setting on the healthcare delivery models with which the industry has grown comfortable. But twilight is not the time to give up hope; it's the time for pause and introspection prior to greeting a new day with passionate and practical action.

A DREAM, A FARM, AND A WEIRDO: *FIELD OF DREAMS* AS A RISK MANAGEMENT INNOVATION METAPHOR

Metaphor is a powerful tool to stimulate creativity—to boldly go. It can facilitate the transferring of concepts dreamed up at twilight into the actions of daylight by generating meaning, inspiration, and recognized similarity. It directs thinking towards a new light, expands context to envision fresh application of existing tactics, and allows mental models to change individual thinking, team practice, and broader organizational cultural norms. It enables dramatically opposed ideas to be placed in the same space to produce synthesis that results in innovation.[11] Metaphor has been an essential part of conveying ideas and seeding creativity since humans began telling stories to each other thousands of years ago. Yet, not everyone is at ease with the application of metaphor; it makes people uncomfortable as metaphor demands thinking beyond hardened facts and figures to extend one's perception of a situation. In the spirit of expanded thinking, metaphors open the mind to new ideas and tactics that target constraints.[11] The presence of the 1989 Universal Studios film *Field of Dreams* in this book serves as a unifying metaphor that will emerge more concretely throughout these pages.[12]

It can facilitate the transferring of concepts dreamed up at twilight into the actions of daylight by generating meaning, inspiration, and recognized similarity.

Field of Dreams as a classic film has its detractors. There are those who might only see it as a film about baseball, or about a guy wanting to repair his relationship with his father. To do so, however, would be to miss the opportunity that its metaphorical use presents: an important discussion about the need in healthcare risk management for change designed to positively affect the broader spectra of healthcare quality and safety improvement.

The American Film Institute lauded *Field of Dreams* as one of its 10 best fantasy films, in line after the Christmas standard *Miracle on 34th Street*.[13] *Field of Dreams* has demonstrated staying power not only as a movie classic, but also as a cultural icon, evidenced by the popularity of visits to the film site in Iowa which attracts over 65,000 visitors a year.[14] The use of this metaphor is intended to broaden perspective and set up a bridge to transfer concepts between the familiar and unfamiliar, ie, to innovate.

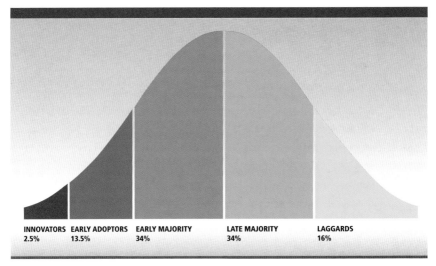

INNOVATORS	EARLY ADOPTORS	EARLY MAJORITY	LATE MAJORITY	LAGGARDS
2.5%	13.5%	34%	34%	16%

Figure P.1: **Rogers Diffusion of Innovation Scale**

The Innovation Connection

Doubt is not a pleasant condition.
But certainty is an absurd one.

— **Voltaire,** *Voltaire in His Letters*

Field of Dreams illustrates that the path to innovation creates uncertainty. It shows the risk that innovators face in taking their visions to the highest levels possible. It models the importance of relationships in moving forward. It reveals how passion and commitment can make the transition from twilight to the dawn of new promise. These themes provide insights for all who manage risk in healthcare and for those who seek their own new way to improve in spite of the risk. Central to the story of *Field of Dreams* is a soul with an inspiration.

Being empowered by belief and having a yearning to find the answer to what is right play out as central plot devices. The protagonist, Ray Kinsella, is convinced of the need for action to move forward on a path that isn't clear but that he feels to be true and good. Ray's action—mowing down part of his corn crop, a harvest critical to his family's financial security, to make space for a ballfield—begins despite a lack of evidence, driven solely by personal inspiration. The status quo is disrupted. The farm is transformed the moment the corn is cut down. Close peers back Ray despite a lack of evidence and in the face of naysayers. Ray seeks advice and champions to clarify and support the action. Learning takes place. A new way of being comes to fruition through inspiration, change, and support.

Ray is an innovator. Contrary to what some may believe, innovation needs a social structure to succeed. The five-point Rogers "Adopter Categorization on the Basis of Innovativeness" or what is referred to here as the Diffusion of Innovation Scale (Figure P.1) provides a set of evidence-based categories and personality attributes that translate the film's characters to the discussion of motivation and need for innovation to manage risk in healthcare.[15(p281),16] Those categories as described by Rogers are:

- **INNOVATORS:** Those who are bold, brave, and venturesome. Innovators aptly deal with uncertainty and setbacks. They embody "derring-do." These individuals bring new information and knowledge into the system. They tend to stand alone in their unconventional views, not always invited to, or even welcome at, the table.

- **EARLY ADOPTERS:** Those who respect and understand the value of fresh ideas and are positioned within their communities to generate support as opinion leaders. Early adopters have resources (financial, relational, and personnel) to apply at their disposal. They can network well and often serve as role models for others.

- **EARLY MAJORITY:** Those who are respected as practitioners but not necessarily as opinion leaders. They see value in new ideas and embrace them after deliberation and consideration.

The early majority are practical and reliable. They represent the cornerstone of implementing solutions and making them acceptable and workable in daily practice.

- **LATE MAJORITY:** Those who are doubtful about new approaches and ideas but aren't destructive in their reasons for not embracing change. Peer

> [Innovators] embody "derring-do." These individuals bring new information and knowledge into the system.

pressure is a notable motivator for this group. Late majority individuals come on board with new things not of their own accord, but per direction from leadership.

- **LAGGARDS:** Those who like things the way they are. These staunch traditionalists look to the past for their motivation to do things the way they do. They don't trust innovators, their ideas, or the changes they strive to put in place. Laggards are comfortable doing things the way they have always been done whether effective or ineffective. They see most proposals for change as illogical.

People like Ray see outside the box, so to speak—an approach that can motivate individuals, organizations, and professions to go to new places. The mindset involves risk; not all innovations succeed, but they have the potential to ultimately succeed.[17,18]

Realistically, some ideas if implemented create too much risk and shouldn't be pursued. The challenge is to sift through novel concepts to discern which are too precarious and which are worth developing, even in the face of substantial uncertainty, solely because trying is worth the risk.

Limits and concerns associated with innovating deserve a constructive voice. Are the limits based on accurate assessments of the situation or complicated by personal, cultural, or even political views? Even realistic perceptions with the intent of the best interest of others can limit participation in innovation. For some, these concerns are an acceptable opt-out for moving forward, but not for the innovator who may be standing alone with an idea. The innovator doesn't want to miss the beauty of twilight or a chance to change the game.

By voicing a different perspective, innovators can annoy. They have an optimistic approach to things. Their consideration of ideas brings an often unwelcome positive spin to problem solving. The belief in possibility manifests excitement. Innovators seemingly throw caution to the wind and smile while doing so. At the other end of the scale, the late majority and laggards (ie, late adopters) tend to embrace evidence as a primary motivator and guide. They scoff at newness, stay the course, and ignore the

responsibility to move forward as needed or support those who seek to take a new path.

Responding to a voice takes time, persistence, and partners. Faith and passion go a long way toward sustaining the interest and energy needed over the extended outlay of work and time required for achieving fresh, exciting goals. Building an ecosystem that allows others to shine, revisit their dreams and realize their goals creates value. Innovation and optimism set the stage for leaders and early adopters to emerge, a new environment and structure to be built, and programs and actions to be designed, tested, and improved to reinforce and spread the seeds of the change.

Challengers of the Status Quo

The funny thing about twilights is that they are always followed by a dawn. Each day brings the possibility of change. At twilight, change can be unsettling and very few people naturally take to it. But change is constant. The innovator isn't intimidated by it. The innovator commits and, through the darkness of uncertainty, presses onward, inviting others to participate. Convinced the new idea will most likely fail, some patiently tolerate the innovator; others ignore or aggressively attack the idea because they feel threatened by change— until it works. The idea shows promise and gains ground. Dawn approaches, and the sun rises.

Innovators challenge the status quo to broaden perspective and opportunity from within their ecosystems and beyond. For example, John M. Eisenberg Patient Safety and Quality Award winner Jeffrey Cooper, PhD saw learning from critical incidents in healthcare differently.[19] As a biomedical engineer rather than a physician, he applied the critical incident technique to explore the role of human behavior in system failures in anesthesia, laying a path toward learning from errors and teamwork glitches that others hadn't imagined. Similarly, Dr. Peter Pronovost has been widely recognized for his innovative application of a seemingly mundane tool: a checklist. He engaged clinicians throughout his institution to apply the checklist in practice which resulted in a new way to systemize catheter use and reduce infection.[20] The pursuit and success of their innovative applications of established aviation practices in healthcare created opportunity for greater acceptance of viewing change differently.

Stanford University is a known incubator for new ideas in research and business strategies across many striving industries. Innovators within Stanford's medical network draw ideas from other industries toward improving healthcare risk and safety ecosystems. The work provides insight for achieving meaningful change. For example, Stanford anesthesiologist Dr. David Gaba spearheaded the application of crisis resource management and in situ simulation training to improve the safety and performance of the delivery of anesthesia.[21,22] He was appointed to one of the first leadership positions at a medical school for a simulation program in the United States. The program has evolved over time to help implement strategies for innovations in simulation at Stanford and worldwide.[23]

Pioneers such as these start with an idea. Like the story of Ray in the film, leaders hear a voice from within and believe in a vision of a better way for the greater good. The evidence and experience come later and foster future improvement in safety and quality of healthcare delivery and outcomes. Meanwhile, leaders are undeterred by uncertainty and risk as they greet the dawn of a new day, believing that the effort is worth the risk.

PERSONALITIES TO PROPEL ACTION: TRANSLATING A STORY THROUGH CHARACTERS

 Screenplays and novels progress by establishing a sense of personality, place, and time to translate a story so others can enjoy it, cultivate insights, and generate fresh ideas from the experience. Well-rounded and believable characters not only propel a narrative forward but can be widely interpreted, reaching across cultural and socioeconomic barriers. As a foundation for this text, the following primary and secondary characters, as well as environmental elements, create the ecosystem assigned to the *Field of Dreams* metaphor. (See Appendix 1 for a plot outline of the film.) They situate the text within the construct of professional and personal motivation to shift thoughts and actions toward innovating the management of risk in healthcare:

Primary Players

- **RAY KINSELLA:** Iowa farmer, family man, and baseball fan who represents the visionary. He envisions, in the 1980s, building a baseball diamond on his property by plowing under a portion of his cornfield to make a space for the 1919 discredited athlete Shoeless Joe Jackson of the White Sox baseball team ("Black Sox") to play. Ray indirectly creates an opportunity to connect with his past, address a gap in his current needs, and reshape his future. Ray plays the role of an idealist who desires change. He personally feels something is missing in this life but isn't sure what, how, and why change needs to happen—until he hears "the voice." Ray is operating blindly—he has a purpose but is unsure of what that may be until all is said and done. Ultimately, the purpose of the change Ray brings repairs a relationship and greatly improves his entire community. As an innovator, he is aware of risk (to field, family and farm), but doesn't let it derail the vision. His

personal motivation enables others to achieve their goals.

- **TERENCE MANN:** Patterned after the author JD Salinger, Mann represents the beleaguered expert who disengaged from his career as a writer after his professional success failed to help him achieve his personal goals.[24] He understands the value of seeking change for the greater good—and he is positioned to be the early adopter once empowered and re-engaged (by an innovator) to gain strength, passion, and courage. Mann supports the innovator in times of uncertainty as he shares the vision. He is invited by others to take on a new role and accepts it.

- **ANNIE KINSELLA:** Exhibiting partnership behavior, loyalty, energy, and trust, Ray's wife Annie demonstrates commitment to the innovator and others on the team working to enable a new approach. This devotion is sometimes based in trust and instinct, and other times informed by evidence. Annie exhibits leadership potential when her values are challenged. Annie has a role as an early adopter by keeping the innovator, Ray, on track. She helps to uphold the vision by recognizing value in his direction despite challenges to the course of action and by maintaining a practical sense of what is real. Annie represents professionals who support the vision at a cost by accepting potential short-term challenges to achieve a long-term gain.

- **SHOELESS JOE JACKSON:** As the representation of the frontline expert in a system that let him down, Shoeless Joe symbolizes engaged clinicians in this metaphor. He serves as a parallel for the physician, nurse, or allied health practitioner failed by a system not designed for human frailty, poor decision making, and work pressures. He loves what he does, feels pride in his profession, and seeks to share the opportunity the innovation presents with his peers. His voice brings the reality of the frontline to the innovation. Given his love for his chosen vocation and position within what Rogers would deem the early majority, Shoeless Joe encourages new players to join him on the field of dreams. He is confident it is an ever-increasing, safer place to play.

Secondary Players

- **KARIN KINSELLA:** Ray's daughter is naïve but insightful. She is the first to believe. She brings a neutral clarity to Ray's vision. Karin is included in the conversation about Ray's proposed changes. She represents the early majority patient perspective and how it informs and shapes healthcare ecosystems. Karin represents those who benefit as a consumer of innovation.

- **DOC "MOONLIGHT" GRAHAM:** Healthcare is built on the backs of characters like Doc Graham. He represents frontline managers of risk, clinical and nonclinical, who are likely to support change once it is implemented. This important role may not be of the mover and shaker variety, but as part of the early majority, Doc Graham exhibits the wisdom of common sense. Given their respect for the realities of the world that the innovator seeks to change, this character can partner with others within an ecosystem to dismantle professional silos and address barriers. Communicating the vision and translating the needs of the innovator to frontline positions, early majority professionals are key conduits for change. They maintain a balance between emphasizing the importance of innovation within their own practices and respecting the individuals with whom they work daily.

- **MARK, RAY'S BROTHER-IN-LAW:** A practical financial professional whose view is narrowed by his inability to see beyond his established mental model, he draws from his experience to do what he believes is right. This individual doesn't see the vision for some time, but once the evidence is revealed, he becomes supportive. Representing Rogers' late majority, Mark is convinced only once the results of the innovation become concrete. Unfortunately, until then, Mark is an active nonbeliever. Mark respects convention and traditional approaches to running a farm. He sees his own approach as the only correct path to address risk, and advocates it as such. His frustration grows as the innovator gains more support. Those who see change from Mark's perspective tend to be uncomfortable with the uncertainties of innovating and can have an unreceptive and possibly negative reaction when encountering a Ray-type character in the workplace. However, after Mark personally experiences a crisis, his somewhat obstructionist approach to innovation begins to shift as he sees and understands its value.

Environmental Context

Context is an important piece of metaphor. Some literature considers *Field of Dreams* to be a rendering of how an innovator can help individuals navigate through their own experience to find a place that is real and meaningful for them.[14] *Field of Dreams* suits the metaphor of managing the risk and safety ecosystem of healthcare in the way it provides a multifaceted view of the interconnectedness of people and their environment as an innovator leads them through a significant shift in tradition. (See Figure P.2) Organizational ecosystems often emerge overtime given the focus of internal improvement at the system level while considering organic, engineered and market influences.[25] Healthcare processes and those who perform them are affected by both the work of the organization and its social characteristics (ie, its safety culture). The right combinations of these environmental elements enable innovation to emerge and change to happen through the action of individuals in that space. In healthcare, portions of the work—clinical or administrative—must have some engineered components to attain success while remaining flexible in order to innovate through creative intervention. In this context, Ray engineers the baseball field within his customary farming business, changing the view of the tradition in this space. The translation of this concept and the importance of place to the practice of managing risk in healthcare and the profession of risk management are central to this text.

Metaphorically, the following elements of Ray's experience in *Field of Dreams* will be used to illustrate contextual influences on innovation in healthcare:

 THE 1960S: Ray's approach to his life, philosophy, marriage, and motivations come from a time when great cultural change was expected and sought in personal behaviors and institutions. The tumultuous decade of the 1960s placed Terence Mann in the ecosystem he needed to effect the societal change he saw necessary. The era gave Ray, Annie, and Terence a shared view of radical efforts toward change. Similarly in healthcare, the rapid evolution of malpractice claims in the 1960s marked a shift in view of healthcare risk management.[26,27]

 THE COMMUNITY: In the film, the community is comprised of members of the establishment who seek to maintain tradition or the norms of practice and see radical change led by innovators as the designs of a weirdo. Healthcare's community is, in many ways, grounded in tradition—some valuable (ie, do no harm) and some detrimental (hierarchy and the hidden curriculum). Healthcare innovation seeks to garner the community's trust. This social structure can either enable acceptance of change or derail it.

 THE FARM: Organizations that provide the space within the management of risk to innovate and collect data and evidence to support improvement. As a part of the ecosystem, they create structure that either inhibits change or enables new ideas to emerge through disruption or designed processes. Organizations enable learning from both failure and success. They incubate creative potential. In *Field of Dreams*, Ray's farm serves as the incubator for a new approach and provides illustrations of value in real time. As told in the film, an innovative organization can be under pressure by the community to conform; The Risk Authority Stanford's (TRA Stanford's) experience in

driving change occupies this element in the metaphor. While not abandoning the basic fundamentals of managing risk in healthcare, TRA Stanford sustains the risk of innovation to explore how that process can be used to create value for the greater good.

 THE CORN: The risk management profession is awash, if not lost, in a field of corn (traditional practices). Traditional approaches to managing risk in healthcare serve as an important core set of actions that, if provided alone, leave today's healthcare industry wanting.[28] These sacred cows, so to speak, can be reduced to make room for practice evolution. Individual innovators and organizations need to understand which customs are ineffective or unnecessary to shift resources—human and financial—with the goal of creating space for innovative system improvements. The resulting space creates opportunities to improve experience and value generated by change. In the film, Ray had to reduce time

> **The risk management profession is awash, if not lost, in a field of corn (traditional practices).**

and resources spent on traditional practice and release commitment to a sacred cow to make room for innovation. Sincere and enabled adapting to new modes of practice—enterprise risk management

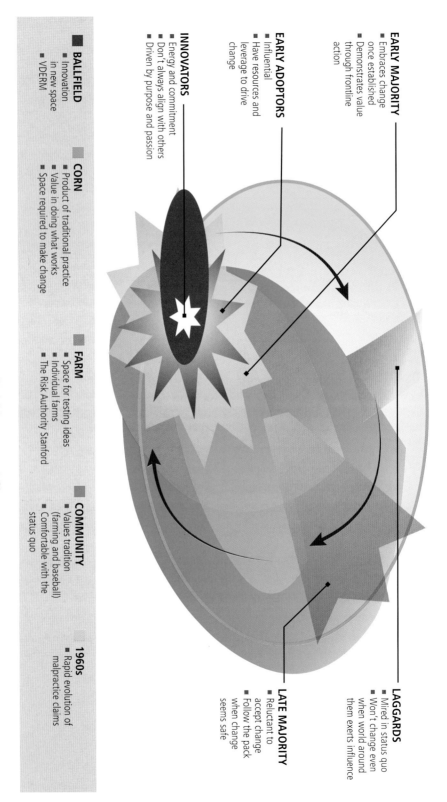

EARLY MAJORITY
- Embraces change once established
- Demonstrates value through frontline action

EARLY ADOPTORS
- Influential
- Have resources and leverage to drive change

INNOVATORS
- Energy and commitment
- Don't always align with others
- Driven by purpose and passion

LAGGARDS
- Mired in status quo
- Won't change even when world around them exerts influence

LATE MAJORITY
- Reluctant to accept change
- Follow the pack when change seems safe

1960s
- Rapid evolution of malpractice claims

BALLFIELD
- Innovation in new space
- VDERM

CORN
- Product of traditional practice
- Value in doing what works
- Space required to make change

FARM
- Space for testing ideas
- Individual farms (farming and baseball)
- The Risk Authority Stanford

COMMUNITY
- Values tradition (farming and baseball)
- Comfortable with the status quo

Figure P.2: **Field of Dreams Ecosystem: A Metaphor for Healthcare Risk Management Change**

(ERM), for example—creates space to build a new field. Risk management needs to plow down some of its corn; to do so will make room for fresh approaches and foster means for the proverbial Rays and Terences in healthcare to collaborate. By working together to clear the corn, managers of risk can increase opportunities to strengthen relationships and collaboratively improve healthcare systems by changing tradition.

 THE BALLFIELD: Creating the best environment for the practice of innovation is crucial. Drawn from effective tenets of ERM, room is made to place its core elements into a space cleared by thought leaders to enable a more value-focused management of risk: value-driven enterprise risk management (VDERM), discussed in the upcoming chapters. The space must work for those who value tradition to serve a higher form of commitment while opening the door for innovation. For example, Doc Graham came to Iowa to play ball in a space with organizational roles and accountabilities that were understood by him. He needed that to achieve his desire and in turn serve the broader innovation through his commitment to that tradition. Once participants in an organization experience managing risk in this way, it is hard to step off the field, as it were, and go back to the status quo unchanged.

PLOWING DOWN THE CORN: STEPPING OUTSIDE CONVENTION TO GENERATE OPPORTUNITIES FOR CHANGE

We do in fact want people to take risks, to strive for difficult goals even when the possibility of failure looms. Progress cannot happen otherwise.

– Atul Gawande,
Failure and Rescue

Ignaz Semmelweis, a 19th century Hungarian physician, was an innovator. His innovation—requiring surgeons to wash their hands and sterilize instruments between operations—was finally broadly adopted two decades after his discovery. Personal experience motivated his quest to understand the variances of post-obstetric deaths from one ward to another. Despite trying, he was never able to fully achieve his vision due to pressures that innovators often encounter: lack of evidence, inability to secure a champion and colleagues with leverage to further his idea, and his peers' perception that his suggested approach was crazy, flawed, and inappropriate.[29,30] It was only after its value was confirmed with solid evidence by the work of more mainstream practitioners such as Lister, Pasteur, and Koch that the innovation was seen to make a difference.[30] Early adopters had created data to prove it. Shoeless Joe had appeared.

Like Semmelweis' circumstance, evidence supporting Ray's belief that his vision had value appeared over time. The long-term importance of Ray's innovation becomes apparent in a variety of constructs, some more statistically valid than others. Two examples of strategies that may need time for their importance to materialize follow below:

■ **Building relationships and trusting partners to see value:** Shoeless Joe's, his teammates', and Terence Mann's re-engagement in their professions, and personal happiness grew given their opportunity to participate and contribute to success. In the film, an unexpected partner draws attention to the first evidence that Ray's innovation is succeeding: Karin, Ray's young daughter. Karin is the first to see Shoeless Joe appear on the new baseball field and alert Ray that he had arrived. If Karin hadn't been engaged as a partner, how long would it have taken Ray, distracted by the pressures his innovation brought to bear on those around him, to notice Joe? This exchange serves to support the continued need to foster partnerships with individuals across the hierarchy to result in professional and organizational improvement. Listening to all who touch an innovation and are apt to be affected by it can broaden success. The hallmark of safety culture nurtures openness to generate learning and transparency.[31] For example, open disclosure programs were at one time considered improbable.

However, with evidence collected and shared broadly by early adopters from a variety of perspectives, including patients and their families, the proliferation of disclosure programs has become stronger and their implementation more engrained in how healthcare manages its response to error.[32,33] Partnerships with patients helped healthcare to see the value of responding to medical error in a new way.

■ **Satisfying the concrete financial and resource needs of the organization:** Translating the value of a proposed change so that late adopters like Mark can appreciate and support its

> ■ **Listening to all who touch an innovation and are apt to be affected by it can broaden success.**

importance contributes to the sustainability of the change. Ray's innovation, once established and recognized by his community, resulted in a reliable and varied stream of income to support the farm. He achieves this by continuing a viable portion of his traditional farming activity (the corn crop). However, if Ray had focused only on the numbers or the idea itself, his goal would have never been achieved. Instead, the innovation meets his personal needs while considering financial goals.

The same approach can affect success in improving patient safety. Early in the movement, there was pushback on the repeated request for numbers as motivation to invest in initiatives to improve the reliability and safety of care delivery. The capital and personnel outlay could be substantial, and the return on investment lacked financial clarity.[34] Yet efforts moved ahead and, despite a lack of concreteness in all work, success is being achieved.[35]

Should this lack of concreteness serve as the example for managers of risk to not seek new avenues to improve the situations of those who are directly and broadly affected by medical error? Struggles and constraints spawn creative thinking to generate and embrace tactics to address those issues.[11] The responsibility of moving forward while continuing to seek and gather evidence and monitor the validity of new paths opens doors that enable the ecosystem to respond to improvement stimuli.

A VISION REVEALED: LEADERS NEEDED TO SHIFT AND EVOLVE

Like Ray who would not wait for evidence that his dreams would succeed before reaching for them, healthcare cannot wait to see all of the evidence desired to evolve traditional practices in managing risk. Its innovators need to be empowered to see a path to build a new field and bring more managers of risk to the vision. It is imperative that frontline clinicians, risk management professionals, leaders and patients alike join innovators like Ray in celebrating the opportunity to build the

ballfield. They need to create opportunities to motivate their peers—whether the early adopters or the early majority—to bring them on board. Through their active engagement, these individuals with their colleagues can generate the evidence needed to proactively manage and motivate learning through the discussion of risk as a component of healthcare delivery. They need to embrace the twilight as the opportunity to begin addressing the challenges within current processes and relationships. They must keep baseline respect for those who strive to lead this work, relish experiential learning, and value relationships.

Do the perils of gaining acceptance by peers, gathering support from the community, and generating evidence of success delay the process of innovation? It is likely to be so. Should approaching management of risk in healthcare from a new playing field suffer from delay as well, while partners and evidence are being sought to anchor the worth of the change in the language most comfortable to traditional value demonstrations? Should progress stall and potentially never achieve its full potential to affect the lives of individual clinicians, risk managers, patients, and hospitals?

Vision and dreams are essential even in light of their inherent obstacles. The role of innovators is to help create partnerships and advocate for a new way, listen to the voice, and right an old wrong.[28,36]

Change is a journey, not a destination.[37] It is a personal and professional reality. The alignment of efforts, motivations and goals with the aims of like-minded individuals seeking change will stimulate the arrival of a brand new day. The vision and aspirations of managers of risk should use the power and passion of a quest to achieve safe patient care and mitigate risk to motivate work toward change. But will all see it? Without evidence and partnership, the ecosystem cannot come to the right balance to achieve improvement. How can healthcare, then, better engage in shifting traditional practices of managing risk to better harness the value of innovation? How can it best mow down the corn?

References

1. Davis K, Stremikis K, Squires D, Schoen C. *Mirror, Mirror on the Wall, 2014 Update: How the U.S. Health Care System Compares Internationally.* Washington DC: The Commonwealth Fund, June 2014. [website]. http://www.commonwealthfund. org/~/media/files/publications/fund-report/2014/ jun/1755_davis_mirror_mirror_2014.pdf. Accessed October 8, 2015.

2. Francis R. *Report of the Mid Staffordshire NHS Foundation Trust: Public Inquiry.* London, UK: The Stationary Office; 2013. ISBN: 9780102981469 http://www.midstaffspublicinquiry.com/report. Accessed October 8, 2015.

3. Landrigan CP, Parry GJ, Bones CB, Hackbarth AD, Goldmann DA, Sharek PJ. Temporal trends in rates of patient harm resulting from medical care. *N Engl J Med.* 2010;363(22):2124-2134.

4. Makary M. *Unaccountable: What Hospitals Won't Tell You and How Transparency Can Revolutionize Health Care.* New York, NY: Bloomsbury Press; 2012.

5. VA Office of the Inspector General. *Interim Report: Review of VHA's Patient Wait Times, Scheduling Practices, and Alleged Patient Deaths at the Phoenix Health Care System.* Washington, DC: VA Office of the Inspector General; May 28, 2014. Report No. 14-02603-178.

6. Shekelle PG, Pronovost PJ, Wachter RM, Rao JK, Mulrow CD, eds. Making health care safer: a critical review of modern evidence supporting strategies to improve patient safety. *Ann Intern Med.* 2013;158(5 Pt 2):365-440.

7. Wachter RM. Patient safety at ten: unmistakable progress, troubling gaps. *Health Aff* (Millwood). 2010;29(1):165-173.

8. *More Than 1,000 Preventable Deaths a Day Is Too Many: The Need to Improve Patient Safety, 2014: Hearing Before the Subcommittee on Primary Health and Aging,* 113th Cong, 2nd sess (July 17, 2014).

9. Allegranzi B, Conway L, Larson E, Pittet D. Status of the implementation of the World Health Organization multimodal hand hygiene strategy in United States of America health care facilities. *Am J Infect Control.* 2014;42(3):224-230.

10. Blumenthal D, Stremikis K, Cutler D. Health care spending—a giant slain or sleeping? *N Engl J Med.* 2013;369(26):2551-2557.

11. Dyer JH, Gregersen HB, Christensen CM. The innovator's DNA. *Harv Bus Rev.* 2009;87(12):60-67.

12. Robinson, PA. *Field of Dreams* [video]. Universal City, CA: Universal Studios; 1989.

13. AFI Crowns Top 10 Films in 10 Classic Genres. ComingSoon.net website. http://www.comingsoon. net/news/movienews.php?id=46072. Accessed October 8, 2015.

14. Aden RC. Back to the garden: therapeutic place metaphor in field of dreams. *So Comm J.* 1994;59(4):307-317.

15. Rogers EM. *Diffusion of Innovations.* 5th ed. New York, NY: Free Press; 2003.

16. Berwick DM. Disseminating innovations in health care. *JAMA*. 2003;289(15):1969-1975.

17. Mittelstadet R Jr. *Will Your Next Mistake Be Fatal?: Avoiding the Chain of Mistakes That Can Destroy Your Organization*. Upper Saddle River, NJ: Pearson Prentice Hall; 2005.

18. Lepore J. The disruption machine. *The New Yorker* website. Published June 23, 2014. http://www.newyorker.com/magazine/2014/06/23/the-disruption-machine. Accessed October 8, 2015.

19. Cooper JB. John M. Eisenberg Patient Safety Awards. Individual lifetime achievement: Jeffrey B. Cooper, PhD, Massachusetts General Hospital. Interview by Steven Berman. *Jt Comm J Qual Saf*. 2003;29(12):625-633.

20. Pronovost P, Vohr E. *Safe Patients, Smart Hospitals: How One Doctor's Checklist Can Help Us Change Health Care from the Inside Out*. New York, NY: Hudson Street Press; 2010.

21. Gaba DM, Howard SK, Flanagan B, Smith BE, Fish KJ, Botney R. Assessment of clinical performance during simulated crises using both technical and behavioral ratings. *Anesthesiology*. 1998;89(1):8-18.

22. Baker DP, Day R, Salas E. Teamwork as an essential component of high-reliability organizations. *Health Serv Res*. 2006;41(4 Pt 2):1576-1598.

23. Youngberg BJ, ed. *Principles of Risk Management and Patient Safety*. Sudbury, MA: Jones Bartlett; 2011.

24. Kinsella WP. *Shoeless Joe*. New York, NY: Houghton Mifflin Company; 1982.

25. Mars MM, Bronstein JL, Lusch RF. The value of metaphor: organizations and ecosystems. *Org Dynamics*. 2012;41(4):271-280.

26. Bal BS. An introduction to medical malpractice in the United States. *Clin Orthop Relat Res*. 2009;467(2):339-347.

27. Mohr JC. American medical malpractice litigation in historical perspective. *JAMA*. 2000;283(13):1731-1737.

28. Hubbard DW. *The Failure of Risk Management: Why It's Broken and How to Fix It*. Hoboken, NJ: Wiley; 2009.

29. Best M, Neuhauser D. Ignaz Semmelweis and the birth of infection control. *Qual Saf Health Care*. 2004;13(3):233-234.

30. Stewardson A, Pittet D. Ignác Semmelweis—celebrating a flawed pioneer of patient safety. *Lancet*. 2011;378(9785):22-23.

31. The Lucian Leape Institute. *Through the Eyes of the Workforce: Creating Joy, Meaning, and Safer Health Care* [roundtable report]. Boston, MA: National Patient Safety Foundation; 2013. http://www.npsf.org/wp-content/uploads/2013/03/Through-Eyes-of-the-Workforce_online.pdf. Accessed October 8, 2015.

32. Studdert DM, Mello MM, Gawande AA, Brennan TA, Wang YC. Disclosure of medical injury to patients: an improbable risk management strategy. *Health Aff* (Millwood). 2007;26(1):215-226.

33. Mello MM, Boothman RC, McDonald T, et al. Communication-and-resolution programs: the challenges and lessons learned from six early adopters. *Health Aff* (Millwood). 2014;33(1):20-29.

34. Weeks WB, Bagian JP. Making the business case for patient safety. *Jt Comm J Qual Saf*. 2003;29(1):51-54.

35. AHRQ. *Efforts To Improve Patient Safety Result in 1.3 Million Fewer Patient Harms: Interim Update on 2013 Annual Hospital-Acquired Condition Rate and Estimates of Cost Savings and Deaths Averted From 2010 to 2013*. Rockville, MD: Agency for Healthcare Research and Quality; December 2014. AHRQ Publication No. 15-0011-EF.

36. Paté-Cornell E, Cox LA Jr. Improving risk management: from lame excuses to principled practice. *Risk Anal*. 2014;34(7):1228-1239.

37. Kotter JP. Leading change: why transformation efforts fail. *Harv Bus Rev*. 1995;73(2):59-67.

PART I: IF YOU BUILD IT, HE WILL COME: MOTIVATION TO LEAD AND DRIVE CHANGE

Innovators are motivated to accept the challenge of change. They listen to the voices that urge individuals to escalate efforts to do things differently, much as Ray Kinsella listened to the voice whispering for him to build a baseball diamond among his corn in *Field of Dreams*. Here, the authors begin by considering how innovation requires both conscious choice and strong commitment, and how it can act as a catalyst for transforming the way risk is managed in healthcare. Ultimately, in order for change to take root and endure, innovators must find the courage to move forward into the unknown. Support must be offered, resources allocated, and a new ecosystem designed to underscore the significance of management's commitment to innovation as it informs and enhances traditional risk management practices.

"IMAGINATION IS MORE IMPORTANT
THAN KNOWLEDGE. FOR KNOWLEDGE
IS LIMITED TO ALL WE NOW
KNOW AND UNDERSTAND, WHILE
IMAGINATION EMBRACES THE ENTIRE
WORLD, AND ALL THERE EVER WILL
BE TO KNOW AND UNDERSTAND."

– Albert Einstein, *Einstein on Cosmic Religion and
Other Opinions and Aphorisms*

CHAPTER 1

PERSONAL MOTIVATION TO EXPLORE THE UNTRIED

Ryan Meade, Jeffrey Driver, Lorri Zipperer

__To seek a new way,__ create a new circumstance, and find a new path to boldness, motivation is necessary. Innovators are motivated by inspiration, driven by a vision of change and forward action that is not always shared or understood by their peers. Therefore, support for the innovators' nonconventional actions is often provided by others who are better positioned to generate evidence of the value of sharing in their inspirations. Thus, innovators must seek partners and create the needed social structure for support. They must draw courage from their networks to move a vision forward in often nontraditional ways.

PATHS DIVERGE AS VISION EVOLVES

In a world saturated with data and calculations, being motivated to explore the untried is uncomfortable and even counter-cultural. It goes against the messaging of the world to follow evidence: avoid diverting from what appears to work. Months, days, weeks, and minutes speed by—decisions are demanded with little time allocated for the reflection they require. Building on the model that is known, the intuitive judgment of experience is easier to follow: it's been tried and tested. It's comfortable. It feels logical. Trying something different seems too cumbersome and risky. Pressures mount to accept the status quo and not disrupt, in the case of *Field of Dreams*, the farm.

Sowing seed in untested ground is certainly not always worth the risk. However, if all remain on their same trusted path, little change will occur. Giving into the status quo trap can hinder innovation and minimize consideration of alternatives to favor a more comfortable course of action.[1] Evidence is a valuable tool in assessing a situation—yet overconfidence in relying solely on evidence can lead action astray. An example of poor decision-making based on evidence is that of New Coke, where Coca-Cola changed an age-old, greatly loved cola recipe—after conducting consumer testing and market research to inform direction. The revised product was released instead to the admonition and rejection of its customers.[2,3]

Evidence and Motivation: a Complex Relationship

The need for concrete evidence as the primary incentive to drive motivation in healthcare is under fire. Evidence-based medicine and evidence-based management are being debated by leaders, innovators, administrators, and clinicians. It has been noted as a factor in the decreased ability of healthcare to rapidly respond with solutions to patient safety challenges.[4] Greenhalgh and colleagues—while highlighting the benefits of an evidence-lead approach to management and care delivery—also reveal unintended consequences of overreliance on evidence. These revelations may minimize the value of experiential or

> Giving into the status quo trap can hinder innovation and minimize consideration of alternatives to favor a more comfortable course of action.

tacit knowledge, delay interest in basic science, and create treatment decisions that were too general for the specific context of each individual patient.[5]

Bias is another factor that can negatively affect the use of evidence in decision-making, stifle motivation and reduce the energy needed to make things different. Using the subject matter of the film, *Field of Dreams*, as an illustration, Shoeless Joe Jackson did not throw the 1919 World Series baseball game as he was accused of doing, yet he was still suspended from the sport.[6] Though he likely took the money offered to intentionally throw the ballgame, he played error-free baseball and led both ball teams in hits, but there was no evidence he threw the series. Similarly, despite a Pulitzer Prize evidencing Terence Mann's skill as a satirist of the radical 1960s era, the film's Iowa community's bias towards Mann's revolutionary ideas almost caused the 1980s school Parent-Teacher-Association to remove Mann's book from the school library. In this pivotal scene, Annie informed the debate by sharing her broader perspective in an effort to redirect the community's thinking to that of a more objectively reasonable one. Annie helped her neighbors see how biases could do broader damage by inhibiting free access to the written word; the risk of soiling the constitution is averted. A similar parallel can be made with healthcare and the management of its risk: decisions can also be led astray by bias.

Bias can minimize the ability to effectively assess risk both evidently and more latently as unconscious preconceptions affect how risk is calculated.[7] Douglas Hubbard, risk assessment measurement expert, points

out that "miscalculations and [the] limited ability to recall the relevant data can affect [...] estimates of risks every time someone asks, 'Which of these events is more likely?'"[7 (p101)] To illustrate this point, Mr. Hubbard used the following example:

> Suppose, if a person is known to have [a rare] condition, the test will return a positive result 99% of the time. Now, suppose the test also gives a negative result 99% of the time when applied to a person known [to] not have the condition. It is also known that only one person in the 10,000 has this condition. In this case, the vast majority of positive results would be "false positives." If 10,000 people were tested at random, there would be about 100 false positives while there should be only about one person with the condition.[7 (p101)]

In this case, overreliance on the test results, or data, would result in 100 patients being misdiagnosed and receiving inappropriate treatment. There is also an emerging literature discussing the problems in the evidence base: how it is developed, distributed, identified, and interpreted.[8,9]

Each day dawns without evidence of what it will bring. Despite data and information to the contrary, there exists no absolute rule that the sun will rise tomorrow. While evidence of the rhythm of sunrise supports that it will be the case, it is not in fact guaranteed. Thus, life must go on expecting that it will until the day it doesn't. The reliance on probability alone is too narrow and can misguide decision makers.[10] There is universal belief that the sun will rise each day. Belief as a motivator isn't a bad thing every once in a while. It serves that role more often than considered. The scientific method begins with a hypothesis (belief)

> Each day dawns without evidence of what it will bring. Despite data and information to the contrary, there exists no absolute rule that the sun will rise tomorrow.

that, once tested, verifies many things, but ironically it can't be used to prove itself, isn't without bias and mistakes, and it can't attest to what tomorrow may bring. The tightrope of traversing the chasm between evidence-based and motivation-based action can be perilous. There is risk involved.

In *Field of Dreams*, the characters illustrate that not every choice needs to be made based on evidence, that sometimes inspiration and motivation toward a desired vision are sufficient to act.

INSPIRATION MOTIVATES

Ray Kinsella chooses to begin to take action based solely on inspiration. He doesn't ignore the voice nagging him to action, to change the status quo. He recognizes and values tradition: college, marriage, fatherhood, livelihood, and farming. The image of the farmer is an iconic one, a profession which is built on the rhythm of nature and evidence. At first the farmer may not look like a risk-taker, but there is a lot of risk in farming. Farmers need to be able to assess situations and then pivot quickly to accommodate the circumstances. Farming is based on the change of the seasons and the subtle calculations of the best time to plant or to harvest. Planting too late could result in a delayed harvest, increasing risks such as an early frost or commodities shifts that lessen the quality and value of their crop. Planting too early could risk the loss of a crop due to a late frost before significant growing begins. Farmers need to manage risk in their decisions by planting in a certain window. But, there is still uncertainty about what will happen during each growing period. Hail could strike at any moment. A flood could leave a field worthless. Insects could ravage plants, affecting quantity and income. Nevertheless, there is a comforting cycle and rhythm to farming. Ray values traditional farming—until he discovers an opportunity to evolve.

Ray hears the voice that changes his mind about traditional farming and inspires him to make changes to improve his field. At the outset, Ray has no understanding of what discomfort he may be addressing and why he seeks a better way. He has no evidence his new farming business model will work. And so what does he do? Does he ignore the voice and his inspiration and simply stay on the familiar path of a life filled with known rhythms? Ray is inspired to untraditional action, despite the pain, stress and uncertainty it could cause him, a notion somewhat familiar to him due to his life experiences from Brooklyn (a borough of New York known for revolutionary thinking) and his college days at University of California/ Berkeley, a hotbed of radical political change in the 1960s. Ray's inspiration urges him to reassemble the very thing anchoring his life: corn. He plows through his corn to create a path and space to make something new. Ray recognizes the lack of logic in building a ballfield within his cornfield and thus dramatically changing his farm. By this action, Ray

YOUR VOICE…

initiates a force of creative disruption.[11] He innovates, against the grain of his neighbors' comfort level with the status quo, and the community scoffs at his decision. In spite of their reaction, he sets a new direction, easing his pain and that of others, to wit:

- **TERENCE MANN:** Ray identifies Terence as a critical participant in driving the change Ray strives to achieve. Ray seeks to reignite Terence's passion for change and radical thinking. In his day, Terence was a trail blazer, literary vanguard, and influential figure with cultural authority. Terence eventually embraces Ray's vision and follows Ray into the unknown and the untried—where he once again finds his voice and a meaningful purpose.

- **SHOELESS JOE JACKSON:** One can only assume the motivation of Shoeless Joe to participate in the transgression of the 1919 Black Sox, but his motivation in coming to the field seems evident: he loves to play baseball. Ray's vision inspires Shoeless Joe to return to the game he loves, despite past negative experiences in his career. His opening up to Ray about the pain he caused himself, what he missed, and his goal to find it again, illustrates how trust and transparency can support the relationships needed to make innovation succeed.

Awareness of systemic environmental and relational influences that impact decision making can serve as opportunities for learning and introspection—a path to a new field. The evidence supporting Ray's innovation to enable this new field of opportunity for Joe and the others required patience and belief despite the risks involved. These considerations are of the kind needed to transform healthcare and the management of its risk.

NEW WAYS TO DO WHAT IS RIGHT

The value of storytelling as a technique to motivate leaders is an established part of the discourse in quality and safety improvement.[12] The conversation on improving patient safety has evolved from one that requires a business case to implement every initiative and program into one that is about being inside the system looking up—one that emphasizes innovation and finding new ways to do what is right, in order to to do what is good. Early adopters need space in their daily schedules within healthcare systems for more participation in improvement work to help them appreciate, both mentally and physically, the value of change. Removing individuals from the work setting, per se for a retreat or even a ballgame, can drive deeper and broader understanding and commitment. Leaving familiar surroundings, or changing the environs where work happens, can adjust thinking and experience to generate new dialogues, products, and relationships. It is in this new space that employees may discover and embrace evidence with a fresh eye to ignite personal passion.

The ability of individual clinicians and administrators to provide justification for stepping off the common path—to propose an idea that may seem to risk the farm—has not always been welcome. However, seeing value in change through the eyes of the innovator helps bring early adopters on board as exemplified in the two examples below. The stories illustrate how taking a new path to manage unexpected care events can generate novel approaches to improvement in healthcare.

Martin Memorial Hospital: Investigate and Innovate

The Martin Memorial Hospital (Stuart, Florida) story of Ben Kolb—a young boy who had elective surgery and instead died due to medication administration error—illustrated a new path to addressing error.[14] The investigative process that uncovered the error was transparent and thorough. The sensitivity of the communication with Ben's parents, and the partnership with the organization and community to manage the reaction to the incident, were thoughtful and appropriate. The changes in administration and delivery of medications in the operating room to reduce the risk of similar events in

the future, and the willingness of the individuals involved to be open about what happened, were groundbreaking. The story became one of the first widely disseminated videos that explores addressing medical error from a systems approach rather than a punitive one.[14-16]

Ben Kolb's death motivated an industry. The discussion of the systematic process of examining his death served to launch multidisciplinary, un-siloed discussions internally at the hospital as well as open discussion with patients, families, and even the media, about learning from errors. It illustrated the importance of broadly sharing lessons learned. The driving force was a risk manager who led the charge to respond to medical error differently from that of the norm at the time.

Stanford University Medical Network: Assess and Respond

Outreach and transparency are strategies that can help eliminate tragedy as the reason to move safety initiatives forward. As with Martin Memorial Hospital's experience, Stanford University Medical Network (Stanford Network), as an early adopter of communication and resolution programs, recognizes the significance of proactive problem-solving. It works to provide both evidence and stories to collaborate, motivate, and inspire others whose goal is to support the growth of communication and resolution programs.

The Risk Authority Stanford (TRA Stanford) designed Stanford's communication and resolution program, known as Process for Early Assessment, Resolution and Learning, or PEARL.[17,18] Programs such as PEARL are more broadly recognized as a valuable, patient-centered new direction for management of unanticipated adverse medical events.[19] PEARL's genesis arose in 2005, amidst the challenge of financial loss from litigation and medical malpractice claims. The program grew from a desire to seek alternative methods to identify and resolve claims before incurring the substantial costs, monetary and nonmonetary, of litigating claims through a lengthy court process. PEARL was established without definitive evidence that it would be successful; the goal was to build it knowing that people would come.

Evidence supporting the direction was lacking in the private sector, and despite existing evidence from the public sector's United States Veteran's Affairs system[20,21] suggesting otherwise, the program received significant feedback that it would fail.[18,22] Much like Ray's experience, the community voiced skepticism due to the lack of a clear evidence-base that it would ease the pain of financial loss. They predicted that the PEARL program would cause increased litigation and insurance premiums resulting from negative actuarial findings. To the contrary, the PEARL program and others like it have demonstrated value to the community in taking this risk. The farm (TRA Stanford) provided a space to allow others to see things anew. In the first 3.5 years after the implementation of PEARL, reported claim frequency has dropped by 36%, yielding a savings of $3.2 million per fiscal year.[17] In addition, patients and families have embraced the program.[17,18] The scoreboard has revealed future direction.

The pursuit of new, improved solutions in the area of incident resolution and learning continues. PEARL is a drastic change in approach from traditional methods in this difficult space. It continues to change the mindset for managing information

Creating space for originality within traditional confines is a tough job.

and response related to these events by drawing from the Massachusetts Institute of Technology concept of hacking in medicine. The three core principles are:

- "Emphasis on problem-based approach;
- Cross-pollination of disciplines;
- Pivoting on, or rapidly iterating, ideas."[13 (p260)]

Since the PEARL program began, it has continued to evolve quickly, building on the creative energy of leaders involved in the work to address problems in learning from systemic failure in healthcare. Given that unanticipated medical events occur in all types of care environments, patients, clinicians, risk managers, and other members of the organization can all provide insight and influences. This can generate improvements and experiences that support both their organization and their broader, professional community. PEARL continues to evolve its communication practices to best address the rapidly evolving ecosystem needed to support the improvement.

PASSION DRIVES PIONEERS TO PAVE A NEW PATH

It's not easy to depend on inspiration and intuition to motivate action because to do so can involve varying risk, from personal, to relational to environmental. Given that, should reliance on either as guidance in business decision making be totally abandoned? Ray's motivation was a literal call to action that he could not ignore. As Ray continued to follow the voice, evidence supporting the success of his actions materialized. Successful innovators trust the intuition, derived from everyday practice, for small decisions that have no hard evidence. They connect stakeholders and cross-pollinate ideas to best respond to where change takes them. They envision the change and create the social structure to strategically implement it.

Those seeking to start anew understand the need to engage others and inspire commitment to the same goal. Understanding how to propel an inkling of inspiration or harness the energy of new ideas is paramount to igniting motivation for change. Creating space for originality within traditional confines is a tough job. The ones who lead in healthcare are those who follow their inspiration and intuition. They engage early adopters through their wit, connections, and passion. Ray's wife Annie supports her husband, motivated by trust and the belief that her husband is committed to a better future for their family. Terence is motivated by early evidence that Ray's vision is possible. While sitting with Ray at a ballgame in Boston, Terence hears the same voice as Ray—"Go The Distance"— and sees Doc Graham's 1922 baseball statistics projected on the scoreboard. Terence supports Ray as an early adopter and commits to the vision to do something radical—to create something better.

Uncertainty causes anxiety; but by the very nature of the future, there is no certainty of what it will bring. Every path has its initial pioneer and that pioneer may have little evidence about what could happen with each step forward. Motivation and intuition about direction can be enough for momentum. This experience will create opportunities for change and improvement in managing risk in healthcare.

References

1. Henriksen K, Dayton E. Organizational silence and hidden threats to patient safety. *Health Serv Res.* 2006;41(4 Pt 2):1539-1554.

2. Gladwell M. *Blink.* New York, NY: Little Brown; 2005.

3. Schindler RM. The real lesson of New Coke: the value of focus groups for predicting the effects of social influence. *Market Research.* December 1992;4(4):22-26.

4. Leape LL, Berwick DM, Bates DW. What practices will most improve safety? Evidence-based medicine meets patient safety. *JAMA.* 2002;288(4):501-507.

5. Greenhalgh T, Howick J, Maskrey N. Evidence based medicine: a movement in crisis? *BMJ.* 2014;348:g3725.

6. Voelker DJ, Duffy PA. Black Sox: 'It ain't so, kid, it just ain't so'. *The Chicago Lawyer.* September 2009. http://chicagolawyermagazine.com/Archives/2009/09/01/092009sox.aspx. Accessed October 4, 2015.

7. Hubbard DW. *The Failure of Risk Management: Why It's Broken and How to Fix It.* Hoboken, NJ: Wiley; 2009.

DIGGING DEEPER FOR INSPIRATION:

- Dru JM. *Disruption: Overturning Conventions and Shaking Up the Marketplace.* New York, NY: John Wiley & Sons; 1996.

- Dyer JH, Gregersen HB, Christensen CM. The Innovator's DNA. *Harv Bus Rev.* 2009;87(12):60-67.

- Hicks G. *Leadershock...And How to Triumph Over It: Eight Revolutionary Rules for Becoming a Powerful and Exhilarated Leader.* New York, NY: McGraw-Hill; 2004.

8. Ross-White A, Tanon AA, Ranji S. Weakness in the evidence base: latent problems to consider and solutions for improvement. In: Zipperer L, ed. *Patient Safety: Perspectives on Evidence, Information and Knowledge Transfer.* London, UK: Gower; 2014:89-106.

9. Steen RG. Misinformation in the medical literature: what role do error and fraud play? *J Med Ethics.* 2011;37(8):498-503.

10. Aven T, Krohn BS. A new perspective on how to understand, assess and manage risk and the unforeseen. *Reliability Eng Syst Saf.* January 2014;121:1-10.

11. Dru JM. *Disruption: Overturning Conventions and Shaking Up the Marketplace.* New York, NY: John Wiley & Sons; 1996.

12. Institute for Safe Medication Practices. Telling true stories is an ISMP hallmark: here's why you should tell stories, too. *ISMP Medication Safety Alert! Acute Care Edition.* September 8, 2011;16:1-3. http://www.ismp.org/newsletters/acutecare/showarticle.aspx?id=4 Accessed October 4, 2015.

13. DePasse JW, Carroll R, Ippolito A, et al. Less noise, more hacking: how to deploy principles from MIT's hacking medicine to accelerate health care. *Int J Technol Assess Health Care.* 2014;30(3): 260-264.

14. Haas D. Moving beyond blame to create an environment that rewards reporting. In: *The Patient Safety Handbook.* Youngberg BJ, Hatlie MJ, eds. Boston, MA: Jones Bartlett; 2003:415-421.

15. Belkin L. How can we save the next victim? *NY Times Mag.* June 15,1997;sect 6:28-33, 44, 50, 63, 66, 70.

16. Bridge Medical. *Beyond Blame: Solutions to America's Other Drug Problem* [DVD]. Solana Beach, CA: Bridge Medical; 1997.

17. Conway J, Federico F, Stewart K, Campbell MJ. *Respectful Management of Serious Clinical Adverse Events.* 2nd ed. Cambridge, MA: Institute for Healthcare Improvement; 2011. [online] http://www.ihi.org/resources/pages/ihiwhitepapers/respectfulmanagementseriousclinicalaeswhitepaper.aspx Accessed October 4, 2015.

18. Mello MM, Boothman RC, McDonald T, et al. Communication-and-resolution programs: the challenges and lessons learned from six early adopters. *Health Aff* (Millwood). 2014;33(1):20-29.

19. Crowley, R. *Medical Liability Reform: Innovative Solutions for a New Health Care System* [Position Paper]. Philadelphia, PA: American College of Physicians; 2014.

20. Kraman SS, Hamm G. Risk management: extreme honesty may be the best policy. *Ann Intern Med.* 1999;131(12):963-967.

21. Kraman SS, Cranfill L, Hamm G, Woodard T. John M. Eisenberg Patient Safety Awards. Advocacy: the Lexington Veterans Affairs Medical Center. *Jt Comm J Qual Improv.* 2002;28(12):646-650.

22. Studdert DM, Michelle MM, Gawande AA, Brennan TA, Wang CY. Disclosure of medical injury to patients: an improbable risk management strategy. *Health Aff* (Millwood). 2007:26(1): 215-226.

"CHANGE IS THE LAW OF LIFE.
AND THOSE WHO LOOK ONLY
TO THE PAST OR PRESENT ARE
CERTAIN TO MISS THE FUTURE."

– John F. Kennedy, Address at the Paulskirche

CHAPTER 2

INFLUENCE OF TRADITION TO SITUATE A NEW HEALTHCARE RISK MANAGEMENT PARADIGM

Mary Anne Hilliard, Elaine Ziemba

There is a certain aspect *of the risk management profession that closely resembles the "If You Build It, He Will Come" theme from the film* Field of Dreams. *The profession, to a large extent, grew from a crisis within the insurance arena. At first, risk managers served as a control point for escalating premium and claim costs, but as changes continued to come fast and furious within the healthcare and insurance industries, management of risk evolved into a more proactive, collective effort. The perpetual evolution of risk management, particularly within healthcare, necessitates taking that collaboration even further by drawing from various sets of experience and integrating ideas from many different disciplines. Seeking new knowledge will drive—or should drive—risk management professionals to build upon the past, question current activities, and design effective, evidence-based strategies that will strengthen future risk management practices.*

THE SEEDS OF CHANGE

A whisper in the wind. A fleeting vision. Prophetic dreams. The inspiration behind Ray Kinsella's drastic actions—to the outside perspective—is unsubstantiated at best, an indicator of lunacy at worst. He has a family to feed, a mortgage to pay, and a cash crop that can support both. Yet, in spite of everything, Ray turns valuable farmland into a baseball field, motivated to act because of something he can't quite put a finger on. A voice urges him to action. He knows change is in the air, knows he must act to bring it to fruition, and so he does. He sets out on belief and instinct alone. The whole undertaking to upset his ecosystem seems nothing short of radical. Then again, isn't this what results in innovation?

All across the globe, in response to ever-evolving consumer demands and practices, industries regularly adapt to and successfully adopt radical changes in their environment. To not do so is to risk immense failure. In just the past two decades, for example, Hollywood has flipped its way of doing business on its head. Film has gone digital; movie rental stores have shuttered, replaced by home streaming video on demand; celebrity can be self-created by anyone by simply uploading noteworthy videos or sharing 140-character messages on social media. The near future could bring the use of drone package delivery and driverless cars. Space tourism is not only an increasing possibility, it is an imminent reality. Despite the undeniable certainty that the passage of time occurs hand in hand with change, most people still experience some level of discomfort with modifications in their world, particularly when they are radical in nature. Even Ray, who followed his gut feeling from the moment he first heard those guiding words "If You Build It, He Will Come," wondered at the change he was ushering in until he saw proof of its success.

LISTENING TO THE VOICE: A GLIMPSE DOWN A WELL-WORN PATH

As described by Rogers' categorization of innovativeness—referred to here as the Rogers Innovation Scale (Figure P.1, page 6), people can have a varied view of even the very notion of change.[1] Ray's wife, Annie, and daughter, Karin, fully supported him and his endeavors from the moment he presented his plan to build a ballfield on his land. Their early adoption laid the foundation for Shoeless Joe's return.

With his family behind him, Ray found the freedom to delve deeper into his quest. He sought out the reclusive Terence Mann, a baseball-loving author whose career had not peaked the way he had hoped it would. Despite the fact the two men were inexplicably drawn together, Mann was not easily convinced. He had to see to believe. He had to experience change directly to realize its power. Such is the same for risk management professionals representing the ranks of the early adopters or the early majority who have yet to actively participate in true innovation to improve healthcare.

From Crisis Comes Action

The healthcare risk management profession started in the early 1970s in response to a national malpractice crisis.[2] Risk Management was a movement birthed in a moment of great need for innovation and the profession received near instantaneous acceptance. As is typical in healthcare, adoption of these reactive risk management principles became the new normal or tradition. Patients were bringing claims with unprecedented frequency, citing increasingly severe harm from errors in their care. Most hospitals did not have established, dedicated risk management programs or professionals in place to address the growing crisis, and malpractice exposures were underfunded or underinsured.[2] The perception of medicine and the expectation of care were different prior to the '70s and hadn't necessitated extensive risk management programs and practices. There were fewer lawsuits, less regulatory scrutiny, and reduced standardization of care. The customary belief was that the doctor knew best and that the hospital was a refuge in which one sought care and cure.

The malpractice crisis of the 1970s— and again later in the 1980s—was no spectral whisper. The nature of the physician-patient relationship changed as a result of litigation. Healthcare consumers began speaking out more fervently about medical error and demanding compensation. To support their claims, patients introduced into evidence their medical records and statements made by providers. Physicians in turn became more cautious about communication with patients. To many, the rise in claims was viewed

> **The malpractice crisis of the 1970s— and again later in the 1980s—was no spectral whisper.**

as an opportunistic assault on medical practitioners, abetted by savvy legal professionals.[3] This view doesn't address the hows and whys of preventable harm in medical care—a reality that creates many types of opportunities.

In response, hospitals and providers created risk management departments and hired risk management professionals, whose principle focus in those early years was to protect hospitals and providers from the financial exposure of malpractice claims. Early acceptance and use was a key factor in sustainability. To hesitate would be to bet the crop. Risk management professionals answered the call by helping hospitals and providers purchase insurance in order to mitigate or stabilize rising malpractice costs. They supported the implementation of reporting systems that could better predict, mitigate, and fund exposures.[4] They stood as the shields to protect against and deflect the litigious assaults.

Early acceptance and use of these practices re-established some financial stability in the healthcare industry, but it did not ebb the flow of cases, nor did it necessarily make healthcare safer. This was due in part to risk mitigation practices which entailed limited and controlled post-event management of information.[5] Risk managers advised clinicians to not talk about events without legal counsel. It was common to take steps to protect evidence at the expense of truly analyzing what the evidence revealed about the underlying situation. Soon it became clear that organizations and clinicians would need to do more than defend and deny in order to promote learning, increase patient safety awareness, and reduce untoward events.

The continued escalation of malpractice issues in turn led to a crisis in the availability and affordability of insurance. New challenges presented themselves. Risk financing was one difficulty but new ways of thinking and doing also became challenges that risk managers had to embrace. The journey continued. Risk managers responded to the new struggles by helping their providers and hospitals to become more sophisticated in their financial management of malpractice exposure. In the early 1980s, several academic medical centers created captive insurance vehicles at offshore locations, which offered more inviting regulatory environments that allowed for flexibility not as available domestically.[6] The capitalization requirements at these locations made it possible for hospitals to self-insure for the predictable layers of risk and to buy commercial coverage for the excess layers of exposure. The creation of these alternative risk vehicles for financing malpractice exposures would eventually influence the risk manager's approach to the malpractice problem.

Once the industry settled into a more self-insured model, the incentives for reducing or preventing harm became more real.[4] The care experience became more closely tied to the business of healthcare. These alternative financial vehicles for addressing the fiscal implications of malpractice were a huge development, but they still did not fully address the heart of the problem. Yes, there were ways to pay for the losses but how would organizations avoid the losses in the first place?

In order for the field to truly progress, risk management professionals would have to be motivated to bring about a shift from a culture of defend and deny to one of open and honest communication with patients, families, clinicians, and organizational

executives about preventable unanticipated patient harm. The fear that disclosure of error might be used against the clinician in court could no longer be the primary concern around that disclosure. New regulatory and accreditation standards created a mandatory basis and leverage for risk management professionals to lead a fresh approach to help others accept the belief that silence was leading to more harm than good.[7,8] Silence was also interfering with the ability to learn from those experiences toward improving patient safety. Most importantly, it was breaking down patient trust in the clinician-patient relationship and the public's confidence in the healthcare organization in general.

> ... organizations and clinicians would need to do more than defend and deny in order to promote learning, increase patient safety awareness, and reduce untoward events.

It was a moment when risk management began to shift its focus to join the patient safety movement.[9] By seeing the process of care through the eyes of clinicians like the film's character Doc Graham, risk managers began to bring to the table the consideration of daily clinical work and the impact that work had on overall financial and patient losses. It was a time when the management of risk started to be more oriented to safety ecosystems.

A MOMENT TO A MOVEMENT: HEALTHCARE RISK MANAGEMENT TODAY

Technology and other advancements in medical practice, in addition to healthcare consumer expectations, soon outpaced traditional models of managing risk. The risk management profession had to adopt new tools, begin to redesign the way services were provided, and address growing concerns about cost.

[PPACA] is no mere plowing the corner of a field to lay down a baseball diamond; this industry shift is equatable to plowing the entire crop to put up a stadium.

New strategies also included increased multidisciplinary collaboration, which would eventually lead to consideration of more robust frameworks for risk management programs, such as enterprise risk management, and proactive considerations of patient care, such as disclosure and apology practices. These monumental changes were disruptive innovations because they completely bucked conventional operating methodology and traditional thinking about managing risk.

First introduced by Joseph Bower and Clayton M. Christensen in the mid-1990s, disruptive innovations are those which create new markets and methodologies, disrupting and eventually displacing older systems.[10-12] Such innovations in the healthcare industry redefined the rules of the game, proving that drastic new modes of thinking were integral not simply to a moment of success, but to survival.[13] No longer could advancement take the form of a quick-fix solution. To work, it had to come as a dramatic overhaul of the approach to managing risk. Growth, acceptance, and widespread use of new systems were met with exponential success, supplanting antiquated standards, and transforming the profession away from one of denial and defense.

Naturally, time continues to pass unabated, one moment after another. So, too, does change unfurl in an ever-evolving cycle. The healthcare industry—reinforced by the disruptive innovations that fortified the industry after the malpractice crises of earlier decades—is currently in the midst of another great and rapid transformation in the United States, this time due to The Patient Protection and Affordable Care Act (PPACA), commonly called the Affordable Care Act.[14] The PPACA, signed into law on March 23, 2010, represents the most sweeping, monumental overhaul of the healthcare ecosystem since the mid-1960s. This is no mere plowing the corner of a field to lay down a baseball diamond; this industry shift is equatable to plowing the entire crop to put up a stadium.

The PPACA was designed to achieve the manifold goals of reducing the cost of healthcare for patients and the United States government; increasing the availability and affordability of coverage offered to consumers, thereby reducing the rate of uninsured care; and enhancing the overall quality of insurance and care provided. The focus in healthcare is shifting from a fee-for-service model, or as it has been called "all you can eat healthcare," to one that is value-based.[15] Naturally, such a paradigm shift presents myriad invigorating challenges to risk management professionals. The shift calls for them to once again rapidly adapt to the ever-evolving industry-wide organizational business strategies or risk being out-of-step and ill prepared.

Today, risk management professionals are committed to promoting "safe and trusted healthcare"—it is the very tagline

> As more and more people start to see the field differently, the reality of the game changes, as does the way it's played.

of the American Society for Healthcare Risk Management, or ASHRM. By the nature of their role in managing and anticipating risk, risk management professionals are expected to adapt to change, including

YOUR VOICE…

new methods of ensuring patient safety and helping hospitals reduce instances of malpractice exposure. The view of the risk management field has changed much like when Annie turned on the lights of Ray's new field. As more and more people start to see the field differently, the reality of the game changes, as does the way it's played.

HACK DOWN CORN TO MAKE ROOM FOR THE FUTURE

For too long, risk management systems were siloed, preventing fully integrated and effective monitoring or acknowledgement of potential risk. Risk managers have traditionally reacted to crisis rather than concentrating on proactively working to avoid it. The term risk has languished unnecessarily as a negative, drawing focus solely to threats ahead, when there are also future opportunities to consider. To achieve a more balanced orientation to identifying risk and chances for growth and innovation, risk managers must break down the walls that have isolated the profession. Managing risk cannot be an autonomous function in otherwise cross-disciplinary industries. Risk management must become more collaborative, a symbiotic endeavor operating in tandem with administration, claims management, even insurance carriers. Enterprise risk management appears to be a long-awaited solution. Its framework and processes incorporate the considerations and

voices of those in healthcare who were not previously heard or empowered to participate as managers of risk. In essence, its focus is the ecosystem of care delivery and those individuals, practices, and places that exist within it.

For example, as recently as 20 years ago, disclosure of unanticipated adverse medical outcomes may have been grounds for dismissal of a risk professional. Today, however, disclosure is an industry best practice, a change brought about by leaders who were willing to challenge the status quo, to be disruptive.[16,17] They listened to the voice; they reshaped the field to make room for the patient perspective. Organizations took the risks necessary to innovate for improvement in the healthcare system. They bet the corn and are winning by reinvigorating the passion of beleaguered healthcare professionals, who like Terence Mann, had abandoned hope of making a positive socio-cultural impact. Risk managers finally have a chance to realize their potential.

Furthermore, risk managers should look beyond the walls of healthcare or clinical disciplines to expand their professional knowledge and strategies. They can envision new realities for their role in healthcare and motivate others to see a new reality through a hackathon mentality,[13] which brings together diverse teams to rapidly validate clinical needs and develop solutions. Recognizing that no one has all of the answers, the more engagement among other disciplines for cross-pollination of ideas, the greater the potential impact and value.

When risk managers accept a role to re-envision the characteristics of the field, they will do so with new and continuously evolving tools at their disposal. One such advancement, enterprise risk management (ERM), will prove a proactive, collaborative approach to managing risk.[19] ERM can help organizations see and understand effective strategies to address exposure across the enterprise, creating a broader array of managers of risk.

The future of risk management as an enterprise isn't merely about ensuring the continued relevancy of the profession. It is about identifying opportunities detectable through the lens of risk. Managers of risk can remain informed about emerging and potential exposures, operating throughout hospitals as the vanguards of risk oversight. Theirs will be the task of strategizing for the days ahead, not simply charged with maintaining the field, but determining how to accommodate a safe, effective place for people to play to their strengths. Managers of risk will seek chances to be heard by their

> **HACKATHON CORE PRINCIPLES**[13] (p260)
>
> - **Emphasize a problem-based approach,**
> - **Cross-pollinate disciplines, and**
> - **Rapidly iterate ideas.**

organizations and executives for a better and more complete understanding of risk—for both exposure and new avenues of success. They will create risk portfolios, assessing multiple potential exposures and objectives. They will design systems for

They listened to the voice; they reshaped the field to make room for the patient perspective.

identifying, analyzing, and addressing risks in ever-transforming business strategies throughout healthcare ecosystems.

Risk managers will ensure that hospitals, healthcare professionals, and patients operate as unified entities rather than separate cogs. They will embrace the message that each member is more than the sum of their parts. Ray and his family underwent a major paradigm shift too, brought about by internal and external forces. When they wake the next morning, they will open their eyes to a tomorrow unlike their farm has experienced before. So it is for managing risk. The opportunities for continued advancement stretch to the horizon, promising a new day with new challenges, and seeing exciting new things as they lead others to "Go The Distance" to build, use, and embrace a better field.

References

1. Berwick DM. Disseminating innovations in health care. *JAMA*. 2003;289(15):1969-1975.

2. ECRI. *Patient Safety, Risk, and Quality*. [online] November 18, 2014. https://www.ecri.org/components/HRC/Pages/RiskQual4.aspx?tab=2 Accessed October 4, 2015.

3. Studdert D, Mello M, Brennan TA. Medical malpractice. *N Engl J Med*. 2004;350(3):283-292.

4. Kuhn AM, Youngberg BJ. The need for risk management to evolve to assure a culture of safety. *Qual Saf Health Care*. 2002;11(2):158-162.

5. Bokar V, Perry D. *Disclosure of Unanticipated Events: the Next Step in Better Communication with Patients*. Chicago, IL: American Society for Healthcare Risk Management; May 2003. www.ashrm.org/pubs/files/white_papers/Disclosure-of-Unanticipated-Events-in-2013_Prologue.pdf. Accessed October 4, 2015.

6. Christopherson, JA. The captive medical malpractice insurance company alternative. *Ann Health Law*. 1996;5:121-143.

7. Clinton HR, Obama B. Making patient safety the centerpiece of medical liability reform. *N Engl J Med*. 2006;354(21):2205-2208.

DIGGING DEEPER FOR INSPIRATION:

- American Society for Healthcare Risk Management. *Different Roles, Same Goal: Risk and Quality Management Partnering for Patient Safety*. Chicago, IL: American Society for Healthcare Risk Management; 2007.

- Driver J, Bernard R. Enterprise risk management and its relationship to the Wizard of Oz. *Resources Magazine*. Summer 2013: 37-39.

- Paté-Cornell E, Cox LA Jr. Improving risk management: from lame excuses to principled practice. *Risk Anal*. 2014;34(7):1228-1239.

8. Council on Ethical and Judicial Affairs. Opinion E-8.12: Patient Information. *Code of Medical Ethics*. Chicago, IL; American Medical Association: 2004. http://www.ama-assn.org/ama/pub/physician-resources/medical-ethics/code-medical-ethics/opinion812.page?. Accessed Oct 4, 2015.

9. American Society for Healthcare Risk Management. *Different Roles, Same Goal: Risk and Quality Management Partnering for Patient Safety*. Chicago, IL: American Society for Healthcare Risk Management; 2007.

10. Bower JL, Christensen CM. Disruptive technologies: catching the wave. *J Product Innovation Manage*. 1996;13(1):75-76.

11. Hwang J, Christensen CM. Disruptive innovation in health care delivery: a framework for business-model innovation. *Health Aff* (Millwood). 2008;27(5):1329-1335.

12. Christensen C. *The Innovator's Dilemma: When New Technologies Cause Great Firms to Fail*. Boston, MA: Harvard Business Review Press; 2013.

13. DePasse JW, Carroll R, Ippolito A, et al. Less noise, more hacking: how to deploy principles from MIT's hacking medicine to accelerate health care. *Int J Technol Assess Health Care*. 2014;30(3):260-264.

14. Congress US, Public Law 111-148. *Patient Protection and Affordable Care Act*. Washington, DC: 2010.

15. This is going to hurt. *The Economist*.June 25, 2009. http://www.economist.com/node/13900898. Accessed Oct 4, 2015.

16. Kraman SS, Hamm G. Risk management: extreme honesty may be the best policy. *Ann Intern Med*. 1999;131(12):963-967.

17. Mello MM, Boothman RC, McDonald T, et al. Communication-and-resolution programs: the challenges and lessons learned from six early adopters. *Health Aff* (Millwood). 2014;33(1):20-29.

18. Denning PJ, Dunham R. Innovation as language action. *Commun ACM*. 2006;49(5):47-52.

19. Committee on Sponsoring Organizations of the Treadway Commission. *Strengthening Enterprise Risk Management for Strategic Advantage*. New York, NY; 2009. [online] http://www.coso.org/documents/COSO_09_board_position_final102309PRINTandWEBFINAL_000.pdf. Accessed October 11, 2015.

"IF YOU HAVE BUILT CASTLES IN THE
AIR YOUR WORK NEED NOT BE LOST;
THAT IS WHERE THEY SHOULD BE. NOW
PUT THE FOUNDATIONS UNDER THEM."

– Henry David Thoreau, *Walden*

CHAPTER 3

STRUCTURE BEGETS A NEW ECOSYSTEM

Ed Hall, John Vaughan, Manuel Solis

Healthcare risk and safety ecosystems *rely on the human and organizational interactions which shape their services, systems, and cultures. Change challenges the resiliency of these ecosystems— whether the result of internal or external influences—as it presents new opportunities, exposures, and hurdles for risk management programs. Risk management professionals, therefore, need tools and skills that afford them flexibility and fluidity in order to stay abreast of the shifting needs of the ecosystems and organizations they serve—in other words, an enterprise-wide framework.*

CULTURE AS THE BEDROCK OF SUCCESSFUL CHANGE

Organizational culture is an important driving factor that serves as a catalyst for transition in ecosystems. Specifically, it's beneficial to improving safety. Organizational commitment to safety culture brings together safety experts, clinicians, administrators, patients, and employees in improvement efforts. It is crucial that healthcare institutions acknowledge that employees are their greatest resource, and that protecting their safety is tantamount to protecting patients. This ultimately translates to not only improving patient safety, but also reduces risk inherently connected to worker's compensation claims, staff turnover, and general dissatisfaction.

Changing the safety culture of an organization requires the active and mandatory participation of every staff member and the understanding by all that responsibility for the change is universally and equally distributed. Instilling the need for shared accountability for safety across the enterprise begins at the very top level of the organization.[1] Each employee must understand their role and responsibilities in relation to the changes being made within an organization and how those changes impact the overall goals for the organization. Employees need to encourage each other to actively practice the methods and procedures that will advance and promote the desired change. It is an we-are-all-in-this-together attitude driven by organizational leadership that creates and sustains willingness to support the new environment and embrace the new field.

Practice Philosophy that Modifies Culture

Transformation of managerial philosophy, inspired by thinkers such as W. Edwards Deming, began in the Japanese auto industry before it arrived in healthcare.[2] New terminologies, technologies and tactics to improve production and reduce

> Instilling the need for shared accountability for safety across the enterprise begins at the very top level of the organization.

inefficiencies—Six Sigma and Lean Manufacturing, for example—entered the management lexicon, especially in the tech industries of Silicon Valley.[3,4] The Stanford Operation System embraces these concepts and allows for standard work that is followed on a consistent is more inclusive and supports listening to employees, measuring outcomes to improve performance, and encouraging experimentation. While the process was successful in many industries, healthcare was an exception—particularly hospitals.

Traditionally, hospitals were organized by a collective of fiefdoms. Each fiefdom was supervised by narrowly focused, siloed management whose view of the overall organizational goals and ability to manage risk in their areas were not its core competency supported by formal training.[8] In such a milieu, healthcare risk management had trouble finding traction to adjust its management philosophy and largely continued on with its more traditional practices. With the future as yet undefined, and an entrenched establishment not used to—and not particularly in favor of—change, traditional practices continued. In *Field of Dreams*,

 each character unexpectedly finds their way to the path of change. Healthcare, in contrast, can proactively engage and manage change along with its associated risks, uncertainties, and opportunities all with a proactive, collaborative approach.

basis and establishes a baseline process for comparison when evaluating efficacy.[5] Other management experts, such as Tom Peters and Steven Covey, began talking about excellence, effectiveness, and management by walking about the work environment and interacting with the employees, checking the equipment or determining the status of ongoing projects.[6,7] All of these ideas supported a shift in the management ecosystem from a top-down directed model to one that

ENTERPRISE RISK MANAGEMENT: ECOSYSTEM ORIENTATION TO PROACTIVE CARE

Enterprise risk management (ERM) is an iterative process that takes a broader, integrated ecosystem view of the business objectives of an enterprise. Framed in a five-step process, ERM improves data analysis through:

- Identification,
- Assessment, and
- Evaluation of risks, uncertainties and opportunities for the enterprise;
- Implementation and
- Monitoring of a plan for progress.[9]

Risk management programs in healthcare tend to struggle with maintaining an ERM process that is fully matured to being proactively—not only reactively—utilized.[10] Full ERM implementation represents a collaboration between the organization's stakeholders, which includes

...the first place for a risk management program to start is within.

executives, employees, and patients, and its professional risk management team. The work brings the expertise of these individuals together through an emphasis on seven primary areas (see Figure 3.1).

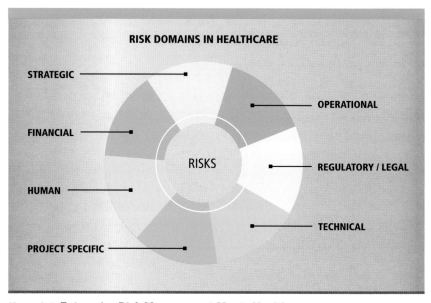

Figure 3.1: **Enterprise Risk Management Meets Healthcare**

When considering ERM as an invigorating management practice, it is important to view the entity in its totality and understand what comprises the whole enterprise. Traditionally, risk management programs consist solely of clinical risk managers and claims management staff. This leaves the organization susceptible to understating potential exposures arising in other risk domains as well as unprepared—both financially and operationally—to address a real exposure. Procedural errors in complex processes can and do result in negative outcomes for patients as well as involved staff. In order for staff to be positioned to mitigate risk, it is important for them to be oriented to the interrelationships of the many facets of the healthcare system and their bearing as individuals on the overall operation. One way to foster this interrelationship is for organizations to conduct departmental risk assessments created to continually monitor the potential impact of real risk exposures and uncertainty in the area assessed on the organization as a whole.[11] These risk mitigating activities should be multi-faceted and involve people and resources throughout the enterprise. Many organizations have talented individuals who are available to address certain areas of risk, but there still exists a need to maintain a strategic framework—and this is the driving force that has facilitated the development and spread of ERM.

Viewed in this way, it becomes clear that healthcare organizations require more comprehensive and data-driven approaches to managing risk; an approach that meshes well with other disciplines in the enterprise. Combining elements of clinical risk management, loss control and prevention, claims and litigation management, finance

> Redesigning ecosystems requires disruption and an innovative hacking of the traditional landscape of a risk management program, much like incorporating a baseball diamond into a cornfield.

and quality to create a more comprehensive risk reduction structure benefits the entire enterprise.[12] Adding space for growth and improvement into the traditional risk management field of practice presents challenges, including bringing together all of the necessary players. It suggests that the first place for a risk management program to start is within. Once there is space for fresh thinking and design among traditional practices, risk professionals can look up from the routine day-to-day grind and generate targeted strategies. ERM provides a strong framework for a risk management program to consider strategic, exciting approaches to inspire shared responsibility for managing risk.

HEALTHCARE RISK MANAGEMENT AS AN EMERGING ECOSYSTEM

How does an organization begin to redesign its ecosystems to better manage risk? Redesigning ecosystems requires disruption and innovative hacking of the traditional landscape of a risk management program, much like incorporating a baseball diamond into a cornfield. In a baseball organization there are different sections: players, fans, owners, coaches, and support staff. For the *Field of Dreams* film character Ray to effectively change his business model, he needed a variety of expert partners, participation, and support of the greater community, plus a new environment and infrastructure to support it all. Similarly, a risk management program needs people with varied backgrounds, such as clinical, administrative, legal, finance, and analytics, plus support of the greater organization and new infrastructure as

well. Furthermore, just as in baseball, this team of healthcare people must work cohesively, respecting the role supported by each area of expertise.

Embrace a Culture of Inclusion to Design an Effective New Infrastructure

There are many stakeholders in hospitals and their interconnectedness is needed to support a changing landscape and a new reality for all involved. To successfully foster an atmosphere of collaboration and

> ...a risk management program needs people with varied backgrounds, such as clinical, administrative, legal, finance, and analytics, plus support of the greater organization and new infrastructure as well.

innovation, risk managers need to create an environment of inclusion in which groups gather to share, discuss, and develop new ideas in a cross departmental setting. This will facilitate the development of programs and solutions to assess impact across the entire enterprise rather than those that are merely departmentally focused. An atmosphere for open and inclusive dialogue greatly enhances the probability of developing relevant, successful, and sustainable programs required by today's healthcare organizations.

The size of an organization will determine how much time is needed to begin incorporating disciplines towards a fully functioning, cross-pollinating healthcare risk management team. Having the resources to more closely manage claims and litigation strategy means more control over losses and recognition of possible risks within the organization. Ideally, it is an in-house function replete with expert staff knowledgeable about organizational mission and values, and level of appetite for risk. Additionally, healthcare risk management programs need devoted resources to initiate, direct, and maintain programs aimed at

YOUR VOICE...

effective loss control and loss prevention. A successful claim program will have a positive impact on the total cost of risk to the entire organization. The lowering of claim frequency and severity will not only lead to lower direct costs but will also diminish indirect cost. For example, in a worker's compensation program, indirect costs resulting from claims can include lost work days, overtime, temporary employee coverage costs, and lost productivity. Rather than simply controlling losses in the traditional way, a new infrastructure can transform a risk management program to a recognized, value-creating resource for the organization.

A NEW SPACE CALLED VDERM: ESTABLISHING ALL AS MANAGERS OF RISK

The current risk management landscape is unfolding into a broad enterprise risk management framework with the implementation of the International Organization for Standardization 31000 (ISO 31000), risk management principles and guidelines. ISO 31000 is a framework for an ERM process that

provides a systematic way to address risk and apply a more consistent approach to identify, assess, evaluate, mitigate, treat, and monitor risks within organizations.[11] It provides an infrastructure for an ERM process that becomes a value-creating risk management process when supplemented with quantification tools, such as decision analysis. Termed value-driven enterprise risk management (VDERM), it allows managers of risk to make good use of critical analytic tools that have been proven effective in other industries such as petro-chemical and aviation.[12] Other tools currently used to create business cases for risk mitigation include the S-curve, waterfall, and tornado diagrams.[13] These tools help to illustrate the total value-protection and value-creation potentials associated with strategic risk intervention programs.

A safety initiative undertaken at Stanford Hospital, Palo Alto, California—and championed by its risk management program—illustrates the VDERM process and its use of decision analysis tools. In the case of Stanford Hospital, data gleaned from the review of workers' compensation loss data revealed many of the direct costs—including lost time costs and replacement worker costs—were associated with injuries from handling and moving patients. A review of the data made it clear that some of the major losses were caused when nursing staff had to lift, turn, and ambulate patients.[14,15] These costs, along with some estimates of savings through injury prevention, revealed an Internal Rate of Return (IRR) of between 20% and 25% over a period of 18 months.[14] As a result of the review, a Safe Patient Handling (SPH) program, a multidisciplinary approach to mitigating the risk of such losses, was put into place. Bringing together the decision makers for collaborative dialogue about the review's evidence—and from it, devising a successful solution—is an excellent example of how various segments of a complex ecosystem can effectively join forces to improve the whole.

During the development of the business case for the SPH program the decision analysis highlighted the additional variables and potential indirect cost to consider surrounding risk and value creation. Value creation is the upside of risk. To accentuate value creation, it is helpful to quantify such items as increased patient satisfaction leading to additional patient referral, or reduced repeat visits as outcomes from the implementation of the program. Ultimately, the results can be quantified by an increase in patient volume and—in

Rather than simply controlling losses in the traditional way, a new infrastructure can transform a risk management program to a recognized, value-creating resource for the organization.

the Stanford Hospital use of VDERM—surveys and direct feedback confirmed these results post implementation of the SPH program. Additionally, monitoring employee engagement scores in pre- and post-program implementation can measure the level of employee satisfaction. Reviewing the program in this quantified manner shifts focus away from traditional risk management to the next level of risk management: value creation—the upside.

Traditional risk management focuses on prevention of losses, eg, reduction in patient falls, a reduction in healthcare acquired pressure ulcers or a reduction in worker's compensation cost. Viewing a decision analysis process in its totality, however, emphasizes value creation. Instead of a simple return on investment (ROI) determination, the decision analysis process brings clarity to the proposed goal of increased patient and employee safety.

Healthcare risk and safety ecosystems need enhanced tools and skills to see a new way forward and be successful in a continually changing environment. Broader consideration of perceptions, from employees to patients, improves decision making around risk which creates valuable opportunities. Looking to data-driven solutions through a VDERM lens will allow healthcare organizations to step ahead of the

> **Healthcare risk and safety ecosystems need enhanced tools and skills to see a new way forward and be successful in a continually changing environment.**

curve and establish an enterprise risk management infrastructure that will position its experts to think creatively to build a new field and improve the culture of safety.

DIGGING DEEPER FOR INSPIRATION:

- Bohmer RMJ. *Designing Care*. Boston, MA: Harvard Business Press; 2009.

- Deming WE. *Out of the Crisis*. Cambridge, MA: The MIT Press; 2000.

- Christensen CM, Grossman JH, Hwang J. *The Innovator's Prescription: A Disruptive Solution for Health*. New York, NY: McGraw-Hill Professional; 2008.

References

1. OSHA Safety and Health Program Management Guidelines, Part C, United States Department of Labor, 1989.

2. Deming WE. *Out of the Crisis.* Cambridge, MA: The MIT Press; 2000.

3. Kenney C. *Transforming Health Care: Virginia Mason Medical Center's Pursuit of the Perfect Patient Experience.* Boca Raton, FL: CRC Press: 2010.

4. Clark DM, Silvester K, Knowles S. Lean management systems: creating a culture of continuous quality improvement. *J Clin Pathol.* 2013;66(8):638–643.

5. Hammerstrom, G. Beyond Medical School: Stanford Holds SOS Training for Physicians. [online] Medical Staff: MedStaff Update. June 2014. Stanfordhealthcare.org. https://stanfordhealthcare.org/health-care-professionals/medical-staff/medstaff-update/2014-june.html. Accessed October 4, 2015.

6. Peters T, Waterman RH, Jr. *In Search of Excellence: Lessons from America's Best-Run Companies.* New York, NY: Harper Business Essentials; 2002.

7. Covey SR. *The 7 Habits of Highly Effective People: Powerful Lessons in Personal Change.* New York, NY: Simon and Schuster; 1989.

8. Zimmerman T, Clark, KL. *Celebrating 30 Years, A Brief History of ASHRM: 1980-2010.* [online] Chicago, IL: American Society for Healthcare Risk Management; 2010.

9. Tichansky DS, Morton J, Jones DB, ed. *The Sages Manual of Quality, Outcomes and Patient Safety.* Boston, MA: Springer; 2012.

10. Harvard Business Review Analytic Services. *Risk Management in a Time of Global Uncertainty.* Boston, MA; Harvard Business School Publishing; 2011. https://hbr.org/resources/pdfs/tools/17036_HBR_Zurich_Report_final_Dec2011.pdf Accessed October 4, 2015.

11. Risk management–principles and guidelines. In: *International Standard ISO 3100:2009(E).* Geneva, Swtizerland; International Organization for Standardization. November 15, 2009.

12. Committee on Sponsoring Organizations of the Treadway Commission. Enterprise Risk Management—Integrated Framework: Application Techniques, AICPA, New York, NY: 2004.

13. Celona J, Driver J, Hall E. Value-driven ERM: making ERM an engine for simultaneous value creation and value protection. *J Healthc Risk Manage.* 2011;30(4):15-33.

14. Forte J. How to build a successful business case for a falls-reduction program. Best Practices for Fall Reduction. A Practical Guide. *American Nurse Today:* March 2011;6(suppl):4-5.

15. Vaughan J, Driver J, Hall E, Race E. A new model for successful safe patient handling programs. In: Ahram T, Karwowski W, Marek T, eds. *Proceedings of the 5th International Conference on Applied Human Factors and Ergonomics AHFE 2014, Kraków, Poland 19-23 July 2014.* Louisville, KY: Applied Human Factors and Ergonomics International; 2014.

INSIDE LOOKING UP

PART II: EASE HIS PAIN: INNOVATION IN HEALTHCARE RISK MANAGEMENT

How can innovators make substantive changes that sustain the tests of time? Through collaboration, just as Ray collaborated with his peers on his quest of the untried. Here authors discuss the vital importance of building relationships, of meeting the unmet needs of others on both personal and professional levels, and of situating the work of improvement in a trusting and transparent environment. It is important to recognize collaboration as paramount to the ability to negotiate transformative shifts in perspective and culture, advance strategies, and maintain a vision-focused mindset in healthcare.

"YOU KNOW, FARMING LOOKS MIGHTY EASY WHEN YOUR PLOW IS A PENCIL, AND YOU'RE A THOUSAND MILES FROM THE CORN FIELD."

– Dwight D. Eisenhower, Address at Bradley University

CHAPTER 4

COLLABORATE TO CREATE
A BETTER PLAYING FIELD

Graham Billingham, Dana Orquiza,
Kim Pardini-Kiely, Leilani Schweitzer

 How exactly does an organization foster collaboration to arrive at a better playing field? An enhanced space is not achieved through the mere incorporation of new space and players. For example, in the film, Ray turns his vision into reality once he earns the trust and support of others within and around his community by considering their needs in his plan. He illuminates the path to a shared vision through transparency and non-traditional approaches to engage others. Similarly, in healthcare, an enterprise-wide approach to managing risk should include the unique perspectives of patients, clinicians, and risk management professionals. This is how an organization begins to visualize and eventually arrive at a better field.

INSIGHTS FUSE WITH PASSION TO CREATE A REALITY THAT CAN WORK

Innovation is susceptible to individual intent, perception, and action. Motivation begins from within, but realizes its true potential through partnering with others to share both the complexity and excitement of the vision. The more challenging the venture, the greater the need to infuse the work with the insights of others, particularly of those closest to the innovation—such as clinical staff responsible to ensure sustainable implementation of it. It's important to understand their experiences and see through their eyes. The necessary partners may not be evident from the start.

Innovators who are open to listening to others will generate insights for collaborators and will employ that knowledge to move forward while seeking lessons from the past to inform a startling future. Silos block opportunity for such collaboration and cross-pollination of ideas. However, risk managers are well positioned to help span such boundaries in organizations by the nature of the work of sharing information and knowledge to respond to and proactively address risk.[1,2] Given that role, they can lead others in a direction that broadens understanding of various perspectives and the contributions that others bring to managing risk.

Healthcare professionals, from the sharp end of patient care to the administrative blunt end, face many challenges while balancing both old and new ways of practicing.[3] Managing these demands through education efforts, communication strategies, budget realignment and reorganization takes a toll on time, funds and staff resources. The toll it takes zaps energy like an illness—"projectitis." Partnerships across the enterprise can be the most valuable resource to effectively meeting these demands. Collaboration improves problem-solving and begins to reshape the field through broader sharing of ideas and strategies. The evolution and implementation of ideas begins

KEY MOTIVATION POINTS:

- Seeing challenges through the eyes of stakeholders produces exciting allies.

- Building relationships with patients reveals powerful insights.

- Pivoting from existing successes initiates support for change.

IN *FIELD OF DREAMS*, the community is connected to farming, and the community, like the film character Ray, has a sentimental relationship with the game of baseball; but the community and Ray were not necessarily prepared for the integration of the two disparate aspects of their lives. Clinicians are faced with a similarly formidable but hopeful change; their professional roles are now undergoing adjustments that challenge the approaches with which they are comfortable with. Rapid integration of new rules and regulations are altering the field they love with new expectations and unfamiliar approaches. They may not recognize the potential for value right away—especially if they have not been oriented to the vision. Clinicians are trained to be critical thinkers and not to believe data at first blush. In order to get clinicians on board, they must be included in the initial design, collection, and analysis of the data. To begin this process, clinicians need to understand the vision in a way that resonates and aligns with their values—especially where there is a lack of previous data that would indicate the strong possibility of success.

through consideration of how best to meet the needs of others—from clinical to administrative. The complexity of transforming a vision into a clear plan is a prime opportunity for risk management professionals. They are called upon to help organizations grapple with the financial realities and risks of building a new field.

Comfortable with routinely donning several hats, risk managers have a unique perspective of each healthcare stakeholder's point of view.[4] Collectively developing approaches to managing risk can guide the way to achieving the desired goal—the building of a new field. Their experience can be leveraged to promote collaboration among various healthcare system participants, including patients. This proactive engagement can revitalize daily work and communication to generate the support needed from those necessary to realize the vision.

ILLUMINATING A PATH TO A COMMON VISION THROUGH PARTNERSHIP

Healthcare professionals share a common goal of ensuring patient safety, improving quality outcomes, and doing the right thing, though they often have conflicting ideas of how doing the right thing looks and what it entails. Effective, transparent communication between administrative leaders and clinical peers from varied disciplines builds trust, supports collaborative relationships, and illuminates the pathway to achieve a shared vision.

The idea of being more transparent with patients and families about care delivery systems and their failures may be viewed by some as radical, disruptive, or even illogical. The idea may seem as frightening as disclosure of medical error seemed a decade ago.[5] As it was then, this

> **Bringing patients out of the metaphorical cornfield and onto the ballfield requires a shared commitment to innovation and transparency.**

Informed Patients

Managing risk from an enterprise-wide perspective should engage not only clinicians, but also patients—the most central aspect of any healthcare process. A parallel to patients can be seen in *Field*

of Dreams with Ray's daughter, Karin: she does not implement Ray's idea but she is central to its design and impact. Just as Ray shared with his daughter, Karin, his reasons for the extraordinary shift away from traditional farming practices, so too should healthcare inform and engage with patients in the redesign of its field. Bringing patients out of the metaphorical cornfield and onto the ballfield requires a shared commitment to innovation and transparency.

transparent approach in communication also requires abandoning the old mode of denying the existence of imperfection in healthcare. Such a revolutionary shift begins with visionary leadership. It requires clinical champions and a patient-centered perspective to sustain successful implementation and management of its associated risks. Fortunately, historical data and evidence show that patient inclusion at this granular level is essential to safety and error prevention.[6] The inclusion of patients in the development of patient care systems may feel uncomfortable or even counterintuitive to traditionalists, but those truly ready to transform healthcare will find it nonsensical to exclude them.[7]

Of course, transparency must continue even where medical system failures cause harm to patients and negatively affect involved clinicians. Forging the path away from denial includes acknowledging healthcare's imperfections. Innovation in this sensitive space can be truly disruptive. Most patients and families will likely never experience a preventable medical error that has a negative impact on or ends a life, but organizations must prepare to help those who do. The challenge involved with designing an effective process will require a collaborative approach and an enterprise-wide understanding of the philosophy behind it. Most patients express a desire for understanding what happened after they experience an unanticipated adverse medical event.[5] Likewise, involved clinicians need support and an invitation to participate in efforts to ensure the same harm cannot occur again. It is at the juncture of patient understanding and clinician support that transparent communication becomes a valuable tool, both for healing and risk mitigation.

Empowered Clinicians

Transparent communication can empower clinicians and patients to gain understanding of what occurred while creating a valuable opportunity to prevent future harm. Patients tend to become adversarial or even litigious when they feel stonewalled by an institution, and legal maneuvers appear to be their best and only option for satisfaction.[8,9]

Giving patients the benefit of the doubt, and the opportunity to question and fully understand their care, may make some in healthcare feel vulnerable. It is the obligation of the organization to support a culture that enables the rebuilding and nurturing of trust with patients and families who are affected by preventable unanticipated care outcomes. Risk professionals are strongly positioned to

Giving patients the benefit of the doubt, and the opportunity to question and fully understand their care, may make some in healthcare feel vulnerable.

lead the way in empowering organizations to define a proactive philosophy and approach for communication among clinicians and patients.

It is important to recognize that most patients are not aware of the existence or role of risk management. Patients tend to have one focus when they go to the hospital: to get well—or at least better. Generally, they are not there to learn about the intricacies of how hospitals operate. On the other hand, it can be challenging for risk managers to be mindful of the patient's experience as they have little clinical contact with them.[10] It is easy to forget that to most patients, hospitals and clinics are strange unknown lands, where they don't want to be. Therefore, the opportunity exists to build partnerships that enable cross-pollination of ideas among clinicians, risk managers, and patients. These relationships should draw from trust and be supported by transparency. Once commonalities are illuminated and people recognize the shared vision, there's still more work to be done.

EFFECTIVE COMMUNICATION WITH CLINICIANS

The traditional approaches to engage clinicians, especially physicians, in system improvements are more often than not ineffective. Skepticism and cynicism—along with burnout and exhaustion from repeated demands on their schedules, even to *do good*, serve to stall improvement efforts.[11] Attempts to create multidisciplinary, collaborative taskforces are often unsuccessful when those invited to participate are not

EXPERIENCE FROM THE FIELD:

THE RISK AUTHORITY STANFORD has created the role of patient liaison, bringing the patient perspective right into the risk management practice, much like an in-house patient/family advisory council. The liaison's role keeps the patient experience at the forefront of the risk manager-patient interface. The liaison is a trusted partner who shares a transformational vision—keeping patient participation and consideration at the center of all aspects of healthcare. The liaison believes in the vision, but has no legal or medical training. Tangibly, the liaison's role is to be in communication with a patient or family member after the patient has experienced something unexpected in care to inform, listen, and address the many needs that arise with a negative care experience. Acknowledging the impact of an event on the patient and their loved ones and setting expectations are key components of conversations with patients. Less tangibly, the patient liaison is an advocate for the patient in legal or review-based discussions, reminding risk management of the patient's vulnerability and lack of legal understanding. The patient liaison fills the gap that has existed for too long in healthcare.

involved in creating or properly introduced to the vision. There is great frustration for many physicians who are coming from an era or an environment in which they had tremendous autonomy to one in which they feel as though they are a commodity. Medical school and residency, until recently, socialized physicians as the captains of the ship, so to speak; as those individually shouldering the responsibility for care, whether delivered well or poorly.[12] It is imperative to move from an autocratic culture to an inclusive one with regards to decision making in the name of safety for patients and clinicians. It is also important to set the expectation that along with partnership and collaboration come

> **Changing expectations is not easy and requires time, clarity, and consistency.**

commitment and accountability. Changing expectations is not easy and requires time, clarity, and consistency.

Though intentions are good, a lack of shared vision arises when time is not taken to address the barriers to change that can exist in groups of individuals from a

---

YOUR VOICE...

variety of roles, perspectives, backgrounds and cultures. Historically, strife in these interactions is brought to the risk manager to solve, which is not an effective use of risk management expertise. An enterprise-wide approach supports cross-pollinated decision making and team-training processes—one key example is TeamSTEPPS™.

The Agency for Healthcare Research and Quality offers medical team training tools and strategies such as crew resource management from the Veterans Health Administration and TeamSTEPPS™ geared to assist with shifting the culture of safety in team dynamics.[13] TeamSTEPPS™ is one of the more successful models for promoting teamwork; but even without a formal program, the focus on teamwork is critical.

Within the Stanford Medical Network, Stanford Health Care's patient safety project TRANSFORM (Table 4.1) sought to enhance a microsystem, or smaller ecosystem, approach to improving patient care outcomes with the use of in situ simulation. The one-year project concluded that safety culture can be improved through a microsystem approach. The project demonstrated that

TEAMSTEPPS™

DEVELOPED COLLABORATIVELY by the Department of Defense and the Agency for Healthcare Research and Quality (AHRQ), TeamSTEPPS™ is used successfully throughout healthcare. AHRQ provides guidance on organizational readiness and implementation. The training is invaluable for patient safety and also professional and personal growth. By creating space for individuals to feel empowered to speak up about safety issues or disrespectful behavior, the model enhances teamwork and communication skills to improve patient safety while fostering personal and professional confidence to listen to the inner voice when concerns exist.

KEY CONCEPTS

- Leadership
- Situation Monitoring
- Mutual Support
- Communication

Source: http://teamstepps.ahrq.gov/

Table 4.1: **TRANSFORM Patient Safety Project**	
IMPROVEMENT STRATEGIES:	**INTERVENTIONS:**
Early detection and treatment of hospital complications	High-fidelity in situ simulation training in teamwork behaviors (nontechnical) and clinical guideline adherence (technical)
Identification of safety risks	Standardized debriefing
Quality improvement of interdisciplinary care issues	Patient safety champion role Monthly unit patient safety team meetings Quarterly interdisciplinary patient safety conference
Individual recognition of exemplary teamwork performance	Monthly award for nominated team member including executive as well as team recognition

microsystem approaches involving multiple interventional strategies—most notably in situ simulation—can significantly improve teamwork and perceptions of safety culture.[14]

It takes passion and inspiration to help clinicians master behaviors that demonstrate expertise in care and communication. For those who are trained to only trust evidence-based approaches, it takes effective communication—which may need to include data—to revive passion and generate executive support to truly transform.

UNIQUE SKILLS REQUIRED TO REACH THE HORIZON

Clinicians are motivated to make a difference for patients. However, not everyone involved in improvement efforts shares the same comfort level with new practice implementation. As shown by the Rogers scale, in any group of individuals, some will embrace change, others will resist it.[15] For example, the early majority will be open to teamwork, training with nurses, and implementation of patient and family rounds; others will rigidly find strength in the hierarchy and reluctantly let it go (late majority). Reframing the conversation to one of organizational values that emphasize patient care as opposed to profitability from the outset allows for consensus building and setting expectations for a shared belief system and mission. Considering that perspective, honoring it, and learning from it will help bring the early majority to the field. It will help patients, clinicians, and others develop relationships that take into account the complexity of how care is delivered and how risk management strategies need to be resilient and respectful of every player's needs.

In a new field, clinicians must also come to view risk management differently. Changing clinician opinions and perspectives will require more effort by risk management professionals. They will need progressive approaches to demonstrate their value

> **It's critical that risk managers pause at this twilight to recognize the value their expertise brings to healthcare teams and organizations.**

across the enterprise. Risk managers—once armed with new tactics—can then seek opportunities to earn trust and build the relationships needed to create new managers of risk.

It's critical that risk managers pause at this twilight to recognize the value their expertise brings to healthcare teams and organizations. It is essential for risk

managers to identify pivot points to head off in a new direction; to discover and leverage triggers that re-invigorate passion, energy, and creative thinking in their profession and present this new mindset in way that it becomes contagious.

Often when risk managers step out of their traditional roles with ideas that are new to clinicians or the organization, they face similar challenges to the ones Ray's wife, Annie, experiences in *Field of Dreams* when she speaks up to prevent the banning of a provocative book at a community meeting. The book is considered by the community to be controversial due to its progressive content. These folks find comfort in the status quo—which in the context of parenting means limiting their children's access to a voice that challenges the parent's view of the world. Ultimately, Annie is able to gain the support of others in the community who align with her passion. She relies on the commitment to tradition (community values) as the bedrock to what is the right thing to do.

The scene is analogous to what risk managers often experience in their daily professional lives. Before transparency became a principle of patient-provider communication, the tendency was towards paternalism and keeping up appearances about the integrity of care delivery systems.[1] To move clinicians and organizations forward in their thinking about transparent communication with patients, risk managers had to personally believe in the new approach and share that belief in an authoritative and passionate manner.

How can risk managers generate the passion and innovation to inspire others and navigate organizations toward a horizon that holds a better field? To continue to redesign the field for the future, the profession of risk management must hire the right people who are motivated and possess emotional intelligence sufficient to communicate in a way that cultivates space for creating innovating strategies within their organizations...their farms.

Risk management professionals cannot effectuate change without also enhancing and augmenting their abilities. The next section discusses skills beyond traditional clinical risk management. To manage risks across the enterprise, risk management professionals cannot limit their competencies to reading a medical record and assessing medical malpractice liability. They must evolve and develop skills in flexibility, operations, and emotional intelligence.

TRANSITION OF TOOLS AND SKILLS TO THE NEW FIELD

One aspect of the current transition taking place in healthcare is the rapid pace and constant adoption of innovation that will inherently bring new risks. Flexibility must be a cornerstone of any risk mitigation strategy in an organization. People tend

It is a true statement in a rapidly changing healthcare environment: solutions today are just solutions for today.

to let their guard down when they think that they have a solution in place—the problem with that attitude is that there will be a new obstacle tomorrow. It is a true statement in a rapidly changing healthcare environment: solutions today are just solutions for today.

To have high functioning healthcare teams, it's essential to consider behavior and personality types; doing so will enhance communication, collaboration, and teamwork. Awareness of what makes people tick and what causes them to shut down is invaluable. It is key to apply this knowledge to bring out the best in a team of people with varied perspectives.

Senior leaders must communicate about risk mitigation efforts throughout an organization to establish the credibility of a proposed intervention. On the new field, everyone must consider the challenges of each individual involved in clinical care beginning with the frontline, a microsystem within the greater healthcare ecosystem. Knowledge of clinical microsystems as the first level of care delivery is critical to staying relevant and being able to offer concrete, doable advice to reduce risk and avoid errors.[16] The next level up is to know operations.[17] The meso level is where process and improvement decisions are made and where standard operating procedures occur. The final level is the macro level—the mission, vision, and strategic goals of the organization. Using this tiered level of knowledge brings value from the top to the bottom of the organization.[16] Building an enterprise-wide risk management framework that rewards flexibility and innovation, in which each individual has a role in consistently evaluating emerging risks, is important. The winning strategy will be organized around the patient. Enterprise-wide managing of risk requires a mindset that the work is never done and there is shared accountability for it.

DIGGING DEEPER FOR INSPIRATION:

- Bradford D. *The Changing Role of the Healthcare Risk Manager.* New York, NY: Advisen Ltd; December 2012.

- Hubbard DW. *The Failure of Risk Management: Why It's Broken and How to Fix It.* Hoboken, NJ: Wiley; 2009.

- Youngberg BJ, ed. *Principles of Risk Management and Patient Safety.* Sudbury, MA: Jones Bartlett; 2011.

References

1. Youngberg BJ, ed. *Principles of Risk Management and Patient Safety.* Sudbury, MA: Jones Bartlett; 2011.

2. Zipperer L, Amori G. Knowledge management: an innovative risk management strategy. *J Healthc Risk Manag.* 2011;30(4):8-14.

3. Reason JT. *Human Error.* New York, NY: Cambridge University Press; 1990.

4. Zipperer L, Wu A. The healthcare environment: blunt end experience. In: Zipperer L, ed. *Knowledge Management in Healthcare.* London UK: Gower Publishing; 2014:35-51.

5. Gallagher TH, Waterman AD, Ebers AG, Fraser VJ, Levinson W. Patients' and physicians' attitudes regarding the disclosure of medical errors. *JAMA.* 2003;289(8):1001-1007.

6. Agency for Healthcare Research and Quality. The Role of the Patient in Safety: Primer. *AHRQ Patient Safety Network.* March 2015. [online] http://psnet.ahrq.gov/primer.aspx?primerID=17 Accessed October 4, 2015

7. Delbanco T, Berwick DM, Boufford JI, et al. Healthcare in a land called PeoplePower: nothing about me without me. *Health Expect.* 2001;4(3):144-150.

8. Wu AW, Boyle DJ, Wallace G, Mazor KM. Disclosure of adverse events in the United States and Canada: an update, and a proposed framework for improvement. *J Public Health Res.* 2013;2(3):e32.

9. Robbennolt JK. Apologies and medical error. *Clin Orthop Relat Res.* 2009;467(2):376-382.

10. Loren DJ, Garbutt J, Dunagan WC, et al. Risk managers, physicians, and disclosure of harmful medical errors. *Jt Comm J Qual Patient Saf.* 2010;36(3):101-108.

11. Lee TH, Cosgrove T. Engaging doctors in the health care revolution. *Harv Bus Rev.* 2014: 92(6):104-111.

12. Betbeze P. Managing physicians may be impossible. *HealthLeaders Media.* April 19, 2013. [online] http://www.healthleadersmedia.com/page-1/LED-291313/Managing-Physicians-May-Be-Impossible Accessed October 11, 2015.

13. Dunn EJ, Mills PD, Neily J, Crittenden MD, Carmack AL, Bagian JP. Medical team training: applying crew resource management in the Veterans Health Administration. *Jt Comm J Qual Patient Saf.* 2007;33(6):317-325.

14. Braddock CH III, Szaflarski N, Forsey L, Abel L, Hernandez-Boussard T, Morton J. The TRANSFORM patient safety project: a microsystem approach to improving outcomes on inpatient units. *J Gen Intern Med.* 2015;30(4):425-433.

15. Rogers EM. *Diffusion of Innovations.* 5th ed. New York, NY: Free Press; 2003.

16. Mohr JJ, Barach P, Cravero JP, et al. Microsystems in health care: part 6. Designing patient safety into the microsystem. *Jt Comm J Qual Saf.* 2003;29(8):401-408.

17. Bradford D. *The Changing Role of the Healthcare Risk Manager.* New York, NY. Advisen Ltd; December 2012. [online] http://corner.advisen.com/pdf_files/OBPI_2012HCRiskManager_Whitepaper.pdf Accessed October 4, 2015.

"THE FUTURE BELONGS TO PEOPLE
WHO SEE POSSIBILITIES BEFORE
THEY BECOME OBVIOUS AND WHO
EFFECTIVELY MARSHAL RESOURCES
AND ENERGIES FOR THEIR
ATTAINMENT OR AVOIDANCE."

– Theodore Levitt, *Marketing Imagination*

CHAPTER 5

A VISION TAKES HOLD

Renée Bernard

 Commitment to organizational values *and goals as shaped by primary stakeholders helps a vision take hold and sustain momentum over time. For risk management programs to enhance their practices to best meet the needs of the organizations they serve, they must first assess these goals, and then begin the process of improvement incrementally. The change could require transformative shifts in perspective and culture, both from within and throughout the enterprise—as illustrated by the risk management program for the Stanford University Medical Network.*

A CALL TO ACTION THAT INSPIRES ALL

Each day healthcare professionals come to their field with grit and devotion to patient care. They wish for a less complicated, more personal space such as they envisioned when they took their respective oaths. Each stride toward this space must be guided by healthcare's compass, pointed toward its north star—patients—with the goal of system improvement and safety.

Over the course of 20 years, Stanford's risk management program has incorporated real-world experience to hone its framework and processes. Stanford Network (Stanford) includes an adult and children's hospital, outpatient clinics, affiliated foundations, and the care providers and employees who create the patient care experience. Harnessing the necessary entrepreneurial spirit and with the confidence and support of Stanford's executive leadership and Board, the program formally launched TRA Stanford as a world-wide risk consulting firm in 2012. TRA Stanford seeks to inspire others to embrace creative and new approaches to managing risk. Building on traditional risk strategies benefits and sustains transformative efforts within organizations and across the broader industry.

Tasked with insuring and supporting clinicians and organizations in the area of loss prevention, risk management can do more to ensure patients are the

EXPERIENCE FROM THE FIELD:

STANFORD HEALTH CARE's Chief executive (C-suite) team maintains the focus of the organization's business of its stated vision: "healing humanity through science and compassion, one patient at a time." Its vision is anchored by its mission "to care, to educate, to discover." The executive team drives a business strategy that integrates the patient as the core focus of the services Stanford Health Care provides. The leadership style is one that never loses sight of the ever-evolving healthcare environment and emphasizes that these changes should not affect the fundamental and essential patient focus.[1] Similarly, at Stanford Children's Health, the C-suite ensures its business strategy is family-centered—which means patient care services for children and mothers are designed to encourage understanding and partnership with the whole family. It is the type of collective visionary voice that calls the healthcare industry to action.

fundamental focus of healthcare. They can make the vision of safe, effective, patient-centered care real. Risk managers must infuse risk management practice with this vision and share it at every opportunity. Risk management programs committed to making significant strides toward this vision will find a way to evolve in unison with the mission and values of the organizations and healthcare professionals they serve. TRA Stanford sees opportunity for a value-driven enterprise-wide approach to managing risk which builds on tradition and translates for use in a variety of healthcare environments.[2] The company's redesign required self-evaluation to identify and assess successes and failures. In its new field, TRA Stanford enhances its program with fresh solutions and strategies

developed with a range of experts within and beyond the healthcare industry. Like Ray in *Field of Dreams*, TRA Stanford sought a way to remove some of the traditional practice (corn) and clear space for the building of a new field and its players.

Too Much Too Soon?

In *Field of Dreams*, Ray did not ask himself or anyone whether he was doing

too much too soon. He dramatically transformed his field, cleared space in his cornfield without harvesting, and plowed straight ahead in a direction guided only by instinct.

KEY MOTIVATION POINTS:

- **Clearing space for new initiatives creates room to think, pivot, and innovate.**

- **Sharing information enables early adopters to embrace change.**

- **Transforming healthcare is hard but valid work; risk management has a role.**

Thankfully, Ray managed to gain support of early adopters along the way who helped him transform his vision to reality. Conversely, Stanford's risk management program harvested its corn by preserving successful traditional risk management functions and identified opportunities to creatively solve its past failures. The transformation was incremental, beginning with fostering relationships and trust with its legal counsel, C-suite, physicians, and professionals throughout the Stanford Network. These bonds grew stronger through consistent and genuine efforts to understand where need existed in the organization for professional risk expertise.

The transformation was not without its growing pains. It had to be rolled out carefully so that change did not occur too quickly and consequently jeopardize

DATA + PASSION = ACTION

Stanford uses data gleaned from claims files[4] to:

- Effectively respond to and learn from near-misses and unanticipated adverse care outcomes.

- Proactively identify causes of financial loss and patient harm.

- Compassionately educate patients and family and manage expectations.

- Routinely design education for care providers about proactive risk mitigation strategies.

collegial bonds. The trust created over time led to an important opportunity to enhance risk mitigation, beginning with the formation of a self-insured program (captive) managed by TRA Stanford. The benefit of managing Stanford's captive insurance is the ability to handle claims directly instead of through a third party administrator, a company hired to manage claims for the healthcare organizations.[3] The increased control over claims files improved understanding of the factors contributing to claims. The data generated provided a basis for collaborative improvement strategies because it bridged gaps in communication with its insureds, executives, and legal counsel.[3] The closer interface further strengthened ties between the risk management department and key stakeholders. Using claims data as a source of truth in communicating with stakeholders about

> Change begins within an individual or a microsystem and requires strategic direction to disseminate information to gain support and successfully carry it out.

needed change allowed for more timely interventions to improve care delivery systems and patient safety.

At each step along the way, TRA Stanford consistently shares information needed for early adopters and innovators across the enterprise to implement effective, proactive risk management practices. The approach, though initially disruptive, drives innovation in a way that sustains the vision of the organizations it serves.

THE VALUE OF HACKING TO TRANSFORM, DISRUPT, AND INNOVATE

TRA Stanford disrupted the status quo creating the kind of positive change in risk management practice that is needed in the healthcare industry. Change is challenging to accept. It can be unacceptable when viewed as disruptive without value. Therefore, the key is to present change in established processes, models, and products such that the value is evident and fosters acceptance of innovation.[5]

LUCIAN LEAPE INSTITUTE REPORTS GUIDING HEALTHCARE TRANSFORMATION

- *Unmet Needs: Teaching Physicians to Provide Safe Patient Care.* March 2010.

- *Order from Chaos: Accelerating Care Integration.* October 2012.

- *Through the Eyes of the Workforce: Creating Joy, Meaning, and Safer Health Care.* March 2013.

- *Safety Is Personal: Partnering With Patients and Families for the Safest Care.* March 2014.

- *Shining a Light: Safer Health Care Through Transparency.* January 2015.

Publisher: Lucian Leape Institute and the National Patient Safety Foundation, Boston, MA.

In healthcare, transformation is a safety imperative, yet it is still slow to occur.[6,7] Change begins within an individual or a microsystem and requires strategic direction to disseminate information to gain support and successfully carry it out. As aspirational leaders in patient safety, Dr. Lucian Leape and Dr. Donald Berwick for decades have led the way in designing patient safety solutions. Their leadership is distinguished by skill in creating and sustaining a shared vision for healthcare improvement. Their collaborative efforts gained structure through the Boston-based Lucian Leape Institute, where they partnered with other experts to define fundamental concepts without which healthcare cannot achieve meaningful safety improvement. The concepts embrace open, honest communication (transparency), collaboration with attention to individual emotional needs and perceptions, and professional education[6] (for more on this work see call out box).

The following are three examples of transformative disruptions contributed to the field by Stanford's risk management program:

Disruption 1: Value-Driven Enterprise Risk Management (VDERM)

TRA Stanford's value-driven enterprise risk management framework builds upon traditional risk management practice with shared accountability among managers of risk from each area of the organization who seek opportunities to prevent harm and loss and also create value. (See Figure 5.1) The concepts are applicable to care delivery systems and business decisions at all levels. VDERM naturally incorporates these concepts in principle and is an example of disruptive change in the traditional risk management model.

For the profession of risk management, VDERM is the lighted ballfield. Uncertainty about a place increases discomfort for most individuals. For example, with rumors of voices, ghosts, and bankruptcy, Ray's farm seems like a place most would avoid. When the lights are on and the players have arrived, the vision becomes clear. The space is soon revealed as a ballfield surrounded by corn on a revenue producing farm. VDERM does the same for business decisions and strategy in healthcare by reducing uncertainty about risk and value creation.[2] This innovation provides a greater chance that decision makers from the Board to the C-suite will have enough data and information to arrive at the best investment strategy. Similarly, TRA Stanford enhanced management of malpractice litigation costs using disruptive innovation and by embracing core concepts of transformation: transparent communication, orientation to individual needs, and foundational professional education.

YOUR VOICE...

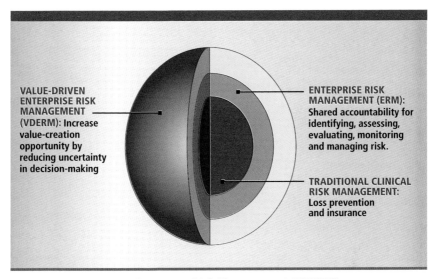

VALUE-DRIVEN
ENTERPRISE RISK
MANAGEMENT
(VDERM): Increase
value-creation
opportunity by
reducing uncertainty
in decision-making

ENTERPRISE RISK
MANAGEMENT (ERM):
Shared accountability for
identifying, assessing,
evaluating, monitoring
and managing risk.

TRADITIONAL CLINICAL
RISK MANAGEMENT:
Loss prevention
and insurance

Figure 5.1: **Value-Driven Enterprise Risk Management (VDERM)**

Disruption 2: Communication and Resolution

Disruptive innovation in healthcare can manage malpractice claims costs that tend to cause crisis.[8] For instance, in the context of response to an unanticipated medical outcome, upending the status quo can empower clinicians to share information in a way that is transparent and sensitive to patient needs. Communication failure is a key contributing factor to patient harm, provider vulnerability, and financial loss.[9] A disruptive approach challenges pervasive perceptions that open communication about medical error increases liability and loss. Fear of lawsuits and liability too often prevents organizations and risk management professionals from leading the way out of a blame-ridden, deny and defend culture.[10] The Risk Authority Stanford is in the early majority who believe the value of implementing an innovative solution to manage unanticipated adverse medical outcomes outweighs the risk.

> **A disruptive approach challenges pervasive perceptions that open communication about medical error increases liability and loss.**

Stanford's communication and resolution program (CRP), termed the Process for Early Assessment, Resolution and Learning (PEARL), is one of six existing CRPs studied and researched at Harvard's School of Public Health.[11] Anecdotal reports suggest that, done well, CRPs can reduce liability and increase patient safety.[11] PEARL provides clinicians and patients encouragement and support to maintain open communication after experiencing an unanticipated adverse medical outcome. A true culture of transparency supports the ethical and clinical duty to treat patients as partners in their care and to continue to inform them of all facts regarding their care.

Importantly, CRPs establish a process for a series of conversations that begin with a disclosure and include ongoing sharing of information with the patient, clinicians, quality and patient safety representatives, patient liaisons, hospital chief executives, and legal counsel. This practice of robust communication increases opportunity for accountability—and most importantly, healing.[12] The success of PEARL is due to collaborative efforts by clinicians, management, executives, and a careful

> ... patients provide valuable feedback to healthcare systems through their personal experiences.

focus on the needs of patients and their families. The implementation of PEARL occurred at a pace more in line with the sensitivity of the problem it was designed

KEY LEARNINGS FOR ENHANCED COMMUNICATION WITH PATIENTS

- Maintain an open-mind for the conversation.
- Set a tone of collaboration with the patient.
- Apply active listening skills.
- Hear the patient's concerns.
- Connect with the patient and express empathy.

to resolve. The pace can and should shift as needed to increase value to patients.

Disruption 3: Simulation and Education

Hacking in healthcare brings together a variety of individuals from across the enterprise to cross-pollinate ideas and explore problems to develop innovative solutions.[13,14] In a value-driven enterprise framework, processes are iterative and collaborative with the goal of ensuring timely use of data and perspectives from a variety of sources. For example, patients provide valuable feedback to healthcare systems through their personal experiences. They have the opportunity to give such feedback directly through multiple avenues, including hospital issued surveys, unsolicited letters, phone calls, and family care council participation. Encouraging patient feedback can generate fresh perspective and opportunity for inventive solutions to address gaps in care and communication. Recognizing a need for improved sharing of information between claims representatives and patients or their families, TRA Stanford applied an innovative hacking approach to quickly meet the need.

The Risk Authority Stanford partnered with Dr. David Gaba, an innovator in immersive and simulation-based learning, to conduct simulation training in communication between risk management professionals and patients and their families. Under Dr. Gaba's guidance, Stanford University pioneered the application of simulation and immersive learning—which includes strengthening technical skills and communication training—to improve care delivery systems.[15] TRA Stanford was provided the opportunity to practice conveying care review information to patients following an adverse event. These conversations were observed by clinicians, risk managers and volunteer hospital family council members. The results confirmed that patients want open, honest communications—especially after they perceive or experience a negative care outcome. The lessons learned from TRA Stanford's experience in simulation can apply to any healthcare setting and in any patient interaction.

DIGGING DEEPER FOR INSPIRATION:

- Chu Z, ed. *Hacking Healthcare Entrepreneurship: A Startup Guide Inspired by MIT's H@cking Medicine*. Kauffman Foundation; 2014.

- Leape L, Berwick D, Clancy C, et al; Transforming healthcare: a safety imperative. *Qual Saf Health Care*. 2009;18(6):424-428.

- Mello MM, Boothman RC, McDonald T, et al. Communication-and-resolution programs: the challenges and lessons learned from six early adopters. *Health Aff* (Millwood). 2014;33(1):20-29.

FOCUS ON THE NORTH STAR

TRA Stanford strives to maintain pace with and, where possible, lead The Stanford Network to greater expression of its goal to keep its compass pointed to patients. TRA Stanford's transformation begins with a vision of risk management as a fully integrated resource. The vision is now a reality thanks to close partnerships founded in the consideration of stakeholder values and needs. Trust grows through open communication about successes, failures, and opportunities for improvement. Due to aggressive and strategic change in the program's design, the space for innovation at TRA Stanford can continue to grow. In healthcare, innovation—disruptive or incremental—can ignite a fire that spreads, but it is only sustained as far as the passion for innovation has spread. To this point, Stanford's vision has taken hold across the organization and there is a shared understanding that the mission is a continual effort and commitment to maintain focus on healthcare's north star: the patient.

YOUR VOICE...

References

1. Roney K. A "lean" vision drives Stanford Hospital & Clinics performance: Q&A with CEO Amir Dan Rubin. *Becker's Hospitals Review*. April 2, 2012. http://www.beckershospitalreview.com/hospital-management-administration/a-qleanq-vision-drives-stanford-hospital-a-clinics-performance-qaa-with-ceo-amir-dan-rubin.html. Accessed October 4, 2015.

2. Celona J, Driver, J, Hall, E. *Value-Driven ERM: Making ERM an Engine for Simultaneous Value Creation and Value Protection*, Chicago, IL: American Society for Healthcare Risk Management; 2011.

3. Greenwald J. In-house handling of claims taps those with 'best brains.' *Business Insurance*. April 27, 2008. [online] http://www.businessinsurance.com/article/20080427/AWARDS03/100024727. Accessed October 4, 2015.

4. Greenwald J. Risk management by the numbers drives down losses. *Business Insurance*. April 27, 2008. [online] http://www.businessinsurance.com/apps/pbcs.dll/article?AID=9999100024695. Accessed October 9, 2015

5. Applegate LM. Jumpstarting innovation using disruption to your advantage. *Working Knowledge*. [online] Harvard Business School. September 4, 2007. [online] http://hbswk.hbs.edu/item/5636.html. Accessed October 4, 2015.

6. Leape L, Berwick D, Clancy C, et al; Lucian Leape Institute at the National Patient Safety Foundation. Transforming healthcare: a safety imperative. *Qual Saf Health Care*. 2009;18(6):424-428.

7. Berwick DM. Disseminating innovations in health care. *JAMA*. 2003;289(15):1969-1975.

8. Christensen CM, Bohmer R, Kenagy J. Will disruptive innovations cure health care? *Harv Bus Rev*. 2000;78(5):102-112, 199.

9. Hoffman J, Raman S. *Communication Factors in Malpractice Cases*. Cambridge, MA: CRICO: March 2012. [online] https://www.rmf.harvard.edu/Clinician-Resources/Article/2012/Insight-Communication-Factors-in-Mal-Cases. Accessed October 4, 2015.

10. Sage W, Gallagher TH. How policy makers can smooth the way for communication-and-resolution programs. *Health Aff* (Millwood). 2014;33(1):11-19.

11. Mello MM, Boothman RC, McDonald T, et al. Communication-and-resolution programs: the challenges and lessons learned from six early adopters. *Health Aff* (Millwood). 2014;33(1):20-29.

12. Conway J, Federico F, Stewart K, Campbell MJ. *Respectful Management of Serious Clinical Adverse Events*. 2nd ed. Cambridge, MA: Institute for Healthcare Improvement; 2011. [online] http://www.ihi.org/resources/pages/ihiwhitepapers/respectfulmanagementseriousclinicalaeswhitepaper.aspx Accessed October 4, 2015.

13. Chu Z, ed. *Hacking Healthcare Entrepreneurship: A Startup Guide inspired by MIT's H@cking Medicine*. Kansas City, MO: Kauffman Foundation; 2014. [online] http://hackingmedicine.mit.edu/wp-content/uploads/2014/07/kauffman_emed_ebook_hacking_healthcare_entrepreneurship.pdf. Accessed October 4, 2015.

14. DePasse JW, Carroll R, Ippolito A, et al. Less noise, more hacking: how to deploy principles from MIT's hacking medicine to accelerate health care. *Int J Technol Assess Health Care*. 2014;30(3):260-264.

15. Gaba D. The future vision of simulation in healthcare. *Sim Healthc*. 2007;2:126-135.

PART III: GO THE DISTANCE: COMMITMENT TO THE DREAM OF CHANGE

E arly adopters and the early majority are needed to bring innovation to fruition. Here chapter contributors highlight that informed and dedicated stakeholders are required to realize success and that respect for tradition serves as a stepping-stone for innovation. As Ray didn't redesign a ballfield but placed a working structure in a new environment, new approaches must be built on a deep knowledge of foundational concepts and the various nuanced perspectives of all stakeholders involved. This commitment will initiate work and evolve process to result in sustainable transformation. Several vignettes are included to show how the power of collective commitment to an innovative vision can result in useful and meaningful change.

"YOU CAN'T CONNECT THE DOTS
LOOKING FORWARD; YOU CAN
ONLY CONNECT THEM LOOKING
BACKWARD. SO YOU HAVE TO TRUST
THAT THE DOTS WILL SOMEHOW
CONNECT IN YOUR FUTURE."

– Steve Jobs, Address at Stanford University

CHAPTER 6

HONOR FOUNDATIONAL CONCEPTS THAT LEAD THE WAY FOR CHANGE

Renée Bernard, Dana Orquiza, Dana Welle

 Respect for tradition serves as *a stepping stone for innovation and can lead the way for risk management to transform future practices. Working toward a more holistic, integrated approach to managing risk is a challenging but attainable vision that can be achieved by evaluating and honoring foundational concepts and then building upon them through innovation. From within risk programs and beyond them, new ideas can take hold where there is patience and consideration of the obstacles that implementing change presents for many individuals. As progress is made and success is achieved, the value created by shared accountability and collaboration can balance the growing pains associated with change.*

RESPECT TRADITION

In the context of innovation and change, it is imperative to explore the basis of current perceptions and practices in order to generate greater success in unifying individuals to embrace a vision for change. In contrast with a sole proprietor such as the character Ray in *Field of Dreams*, organizations that simply mow down traditional practice without full understanding of its relevance to daily work may stifle the ability to share and sustain a new vision. The stakeholders in an organization must come to understand that the dream of bringing innovation to fruition begins with a clear understanding of the context within which present views and practices emerge. They must understand that they should look back to connect the dots, to innovate.

Not long ago today's commonplace items—the light bulb, penicillin, the telephone—represented innovation. Within the last century, inventions have improved and shaped the world. Much to the relief and joy of their parents, children with infections that were once untreatable are now cured with penicillin. Separated families who once had to wait days, weeks and months before receiving letters from around the globe are now connecting instantly over video chat. Much progress has been made since the days of the Pony Express. As innovations rapidly change around the world, one thing remains constant: the challenge of proposing something radically different. New ideas may fail simply due to resistance to change.

Healthcare and its risks and opportunities continue to evolve. Acknowledging that foundational influences of its evolution are closely tied to individuals, their perceptions, and their needs within the system, will help foster and maintain enthusiasm for the change to further promote improvement. A longitudinal study by the National Science Foundation concluded that the key to having employees who are both satisfied and productive is motivation.[1] Personal motivation arises from individual commitment to the proposed idea, an important factor to consider when introducing change.[1]

KEY MOTIVATION POINTS:

- Listening to multiple voices can keep the innovation spirit alive.

- Evolving practice creates energy and space for change.

- Building relationships helps to go the distance.

Those in healthcare share a common commitment to providing patient care in the safest and most satisfying way possible; traditional procedures in daily routines can often block that shared commitment. In *Field of Dreams*, the corn obscured the view of a more exciting and fulfilling field. In healthcare, innovators and early adopters have the seeds of new ideas they would like to sow. However, their ideas can get marginalized by the complexity of healthcare systems that cannot enable the necessary time and resources needed to cultivate meaningful change. In such a space, passion subsides quickly, crushing the spirit of innovation. It is imperative that many voices work together to keep the spirit of innovation alive and thriving.

VALUE DIVERSE IDEAS

Honoring and expressing genuine appreciation for the value of diverse ideas will facilitate innovation and growth. Everyone must have the opportunity to develop a voice so they can join the discussion in the innovative space about the design of the new field.

Risk managers have a prime opportunity to exemplify the concept of thinking outside of tradition. Each day brings a possibility to broaden perceptions—both their own views and those of whom they serve— around what it means to collaboratively

> **FOUNDATIONAL CONCEPTS FOR INNOVATIVE CHANGE**
>
> - **Respect tradition**
> - **Value diverse ideas**
> - **View disruptive innovation positively**
> - **Prepare the next generation**
> - **Invest in the future**
> - **Nurture and honor relationships**

manage risk. Incrementally, risk managers need leadership support for creating space within their daily work demands to delve into the kind of visionary inspiration and motivation that moves organizations up the scale from "good to great," to use Collins's phrase.[2] Unpredictable risk events which cannot be proactively mitigated will always exist. However, building flexibility and space for innovation into the organizational infrastructure will improve the ability to react effectively—both internally and in the greater community.

A storm of change is swirling about healthcare. To the ordinary eye, controlling the steeply rising cost of care while simultaneously improving the field appears to be a contradiction. However, fiscal responsibility and fostering care improvement are part of routine practice in the risk management profession. The key is to quickly seek out new and innovative ways to better manage risk. As healthcare processes continue to shift in growth and improvement, strategies also need to balance management of associated risks with meeting patient needs and maintaining fiscal value.[2]

VIEW DISRUPTIVE INNOVATION POSITIVELY

The risk management profession will have to rise to the occasion and proactively respond to the need for change, rather than react to the negative impact of unmitigated risk. Like a phoenix rising from the ashes of its predecessor, risk professionals have the opportunity to breathe life into their practice and bring others to the new field. The evolution of the practice of risk management is shifting from focusing on protecting financial assets (value protection) to a broader value-creating role intended to perpetuate patient safety—enterprise risk management, wherein each member of an organization is a manager of risk. (See Figure 6.1)

How can risk managers grab opportunity in the presence of uncertainty, skepticism, and limited resources? They need a skillful balance of traditional practice and room in their hectic schedules to reflect, innovate, and generate fresh solutions to maximize the value of routine while anticipating risk.

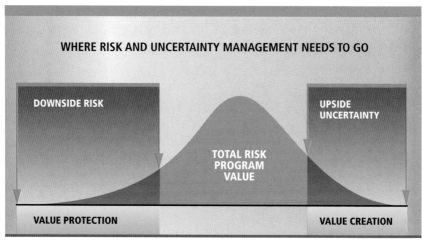

Credit: TRA Stanford

Figure 6.1: **Beyond Traditional Risk Management**

Despite the transition that organizations are making toward enterprise risk management, too many risk managers are spending a great deal of time in reactionary mode, stretched too thin across a variety of different titles and responsibilities. Under such circumstances, it is difficult to break into new areas of the enterprise and advance education around managing risk from the bottom up and the top down, from the bedside to outpatient settings. For example, a system-oriented review of the facts of a wrong medication event

> **Despite the transition that organizations are making toward enterprise risk management, too many risk managers are spending a great deal of time in reactionary mode, stretched too thin across a variety of different titles and responsibilities.**

takes time; it can take several weeks to complete chart reviews, hold interviews, run root cause analysis (RCA), and perform an assessment of liability and damages. Limited resources and constraints on time strongly affect the ability of risk managers to proactively identify risk across the organization. Instead they deal with only those situations that need their immediate attention and then move on to the next issue that then needs their immediate attention—somewhat like a healthcare version of the game of whack-a-mole. One innovative solution is to consider bringing a more diverse skillset to the profession to

continue the vision of evolving practices for managing risk.

PREPARE THE NEXT GENERATION

Adherence to traditional hiring practices for risk mangers results in a narrow or underutilized skillset that is insufficient for proactively managing organizational risks in today's dynamic and ecosystem-oriented care environment.[4] The traditional rationale in hiring risk managers is that those with clinical expertise have better capability for quickly reviewing medical charts for standard of care and process issues, navigating through the hospital system, and engaging with other clinicians to discuss their findings. The reality is that what today's healthcare system needs from risk management has evolved as the business and what consumers expect from it has become more complex.[5]

The next generation of risk professionals should be specialists with varied backgrounds, (insurance, patient safety, workers compensation, risk finance) with cross-functional capabilities. Strategic thinking, planning, and leadership are skills necessary for making enterprise-wide change happen.[6] The concept of hiring to grow and hiring for fit may seem as crazy as Ray's vision of turning part of his farm into a baseball field. Making meaningful change requires an appropriate skillset to lead healthcare risk management into the next decade and beyond.[6] Perhaps it's time to shift mindset? Does holding a specific degree in either nursing or law make a better candidate for the risk management role? Perhaps it's time to think about considering candidates outside of nursing and law who demonstrate skill and culture fit? For example, by traditional hiring practices, an individual with a master's degree in a healthcare domain who does not have clinical experience may be excluded from a list of potential job candidates. That person may very well have the skillset and cultural fit to manage risk, but the organization will never know since the individual was not afforded the opportunity to demonstrate their capabilities via interview or other modes of candidate selection.

Healthcare organizations might consider hiring people with different experience and ideas with an eye toward whether or not those experiences complement the team. The prioritization of fit first creates a responsibility to consider emotional, generational, and organizational culture barriers when interacting with executives, clinicians, and patients who have

EXPERIENCE FROM THE FIELD:

THE RISK AUTHORITY STANFORD RECOGNIZES that creative, passionate, energetic, inquisitive, and self-motivated individuals can develop and thrive in an environment whose credo and culture encourage staff to:

- Support each other,
- Communicate in person, rather than email,
- Use cross-functional inter-department teams,
- Begin statements with declared intention,
- Be flexible and adapt accordingly,
- Exhibit accountability for role and shared-vision,
- Express gratitude for colleagues,
- Work to find shared truths with colleagues,
- Routinely debrief to assess what works and what does not.

traditionally been placed in silos within healthcare.

Change in hiring practices is a form of self-evaluation and a key step to implementing an enterprise risk management framework. With new leaders bent towards efficiency, growth, and innovation, risk management programs can change their culture and practices by infusing a variety of perspectives among their staff. For example, Ray came to farming having explored firsthand 1960s revolutionary thinking while in college in California. He was shaped by those experiences and therefore not intimidated to bring out-of-the box thinking to his small farm in Iowa. Broader perspectives will more likely result in a program with busy, but productive and satisfied individuals who push each other to excellence and open the door to new ways of thinking. Such are the kinds of results that echo the principle and belief that risk management professionals can perform their traditional functions and still enjoy the fruits of creative, professional labor.[6]

Just as personal and professional mindfulness is fostered through first-hand experience, maintaining an innovative vision requires ongoing knowledge sharing and interactions where the work and action takes place.

Traditionally, those clinicians who are brought into the profession of healthcare risk management obtain professional certification in healthcare risk management (CPHRM status).[7] The certification is valuable to risk managers just as a medical education is to physicians. Much like the field of medicine sends its students and trainees to clinical settings around the country, so too must risk professionals be immersed in new environments.

INVEST IN THE FUTURE

Tell me and I forget. Teach me and I remember. Involve me and I learn.
    – Xunzi, *Ruxiao*

Risk professionals come from a variety of diverse educational backgrounds, such as nursing, insurance, healthcare administration, and law. Each of these backgrounds brings unique perspectives and approaches to managing risk. Education in healthcare risk management is obtained from experience, as well as continuing education classes and certifications provided through the American Society for Healthcare Risk Management (ASHRM). Risk management education is essential, particularly in today's rapidly changing environment. New regulations and laws bring greater complexity to an already challenging environment. Emergent technology may have unrealized intrinsic risk (latent risk) and innovative healthcare models may be changing the delivery of healthcare.

A combination of education, application, problem solving, and experience make a significant impact on the healthcare worker when transitioning from student to professional and progressing from novice to expert. Professions such as nursing and medicine have augmented foundational education through residency programs, while other professionals enter the workforce after completing requisite licensure requirements and employee orientation. Many skills are acquired on the job through trial and error.[8]

Risk Management in Residency

The Risk Authority Stanford recognizes the wealth of education and experience from professionals representing a wide variety of disciplines. Many risk managers simply fell into the work of risk management rather than taking a focused, linear path to it. Whether falling into it or directly pursuing it, risk management can be a daunting experience. Competing priorities, time constraints, stress, and organizational complexities can be substantial challenges to any professional.

There are opportunities to make a positive impact in risk management by linking competencies to professional development through supplemental education and training.

At The Risk Authority Stanford, the educational philosophy is to deliver broad, high quality education and training in a safe, academic, and collegial environment. The mission and goals of the TRA Stanford Risk Manager in Residency program are to foster an atmosphere of intellectual curiosity where participants can consistently apply their problem solving and social interaction skills. Through simulation, case studies, and self-reflective exercises, risk management professionals have the opportunity to learn, stretch, and grow into the highly skilled professionals they desire to be and which are needed to engage organizational stakeholders who can support and enable transformation of a risk management program. Engagement creates new opportunities to build trust and confidence in the value risk management can produce in a multitude of ways for an organization.

NURTURE AND HONOR RELATIONSHIPS

In healthcare risk management, one way to build confidence and trust is to understand the perspectives of physicians and how they may typically view interactions

STANFORD COMMITTEE FOR PROFESSIONAL SATISFACTION AND SUPPORT (SCPSS)[10]

Peer support programs are designed to train a team of providers who can then reach out to colleagues to offer support and guidance through difficult events. Physicians often do not reach out for—or recognize they need—support and as a result underutilize traditional support mechanisms, such as employee assistance or faculty assistance programs. Stanford Health Care's peer support program offers peer assistance to practitioners in need of support by connecting them with physicians who have experienced such similar circumstances and can truly understand and help the provider heal. SCPSS promotes or sponsors efforts at Stanford to improve:

- Personal health (prevention and healthy behaviors),
- Organizational and peer support,
- Community building and colleagueship,
- Work-life integration,
- Personal resilience and professional satisfaction,
- Organizational and personal values alignment.

with risk management. Traditionally, the perception of needing risk management consultation is sorrowful and what most might consider a bad day. When a physician needs assistance from risk management it is usually because some part of patient care has gone or is going awry. Difficult outcomes can cause a clinician to have self-doubt, to have fear of repeating the error, to leave the profession, or to end in self-harm. A 2007 study of over 3,000 physicians determined that less than 10% of those involved in difficult events felt supported by their institutions.[9] Progressive risk mitigation strategies around unanticipated adverse care outcomes recognize the impact these events have on clinicians. They recognize the importance of establishing

emotional support systems both within and outside the organization. Such strategies are leading to physician peer support programs gaining traction as the right thing to do for physicians. The Risk Authority Stanford has partnered with Stanford Network physician leadership to promote or sponsor efforts to improve physician and clinician wellness.

> If risk professionals are to help bring organizational goals and visions to fruition, it is vital to have an understanding of the values others bring to the work and the foundational concepts that support them.

Healthcare organizations, with the support of risk managers, are responding to mitigate the safety risks associated with physician dissatisfaction and lack of peer support.[11] Establishing a process to generate immediate referral for

DIGGING DEEPER FOR INSPIRATION:

- Driver J, Bernard R. Enterprise risk management and its relationship to the Wizard of Oz. *Resources Magazine.* 2013;Summer:37-39.

- Furr N, Dyer JH. Leading your team into the unknown: how great managers empower their organizations to innovate. *Harv Bus Rev.* 2014;92(12):80-88.

- Gladwell M. *David and Goliath: Underdogs, Misfits, and the Art of Battling Giants.* Boston, MA: Little, Brown and Company; 2013.

emotional support after difficult events is just one important step that can help change the perception of the value risk management brings to its organizations. If risk professionals are to help bring organizational goals and visions to fruition, it is vital to have an understanding of the values others bring to the work and the foundational concepts that support them. Risk professionals have similar alliance opportunities due to their traditional functions which require interactions with key stakeholders. Delving further into those alliances to drive exploration of new approaches for managing risk in healthcare can lead to innovative change in the broader industry.

References:

1. Petra T. Improve commitment by understanding the personal nature of motivation. *The Fordyce Letter.* June 12, 2014. [online] http://www.eremedia.com/fordyce/improve-commitment-by-understanding-the-personal-nature-of-motivation/. Accessed October 4, 2015.

2. Collins J. *Good to Great: Why Some Companies Make the Leap and Others Don't.* New York, NY: Harper Business; 2001.

3. Bradford D. *The Changing Role of the Healthcare Risk Manager.* New York, NY. Advisen Ltd; December 2012. [online] http://corner.advisen.com/pdf_files/OBPI_2012HCRiskManager_Whitepaper.pdf. Accessed October 4, 2015.

4. Napier J, Youngberg B. Risk management and patient safety: the synergy and the tension. In: Youngberg B, ed. *Principles of Risk Management and Patient Safety.* Sudbury, MA: Jones Bartlett; 2011:3-11.

5. ECRI. *Patient Safety, Risk, and Quality.* November 18, 2104. [online] https://www.ecri.org/components/HRC/Pages/RiskQual4.aspx?tab=2 Accessed October 10, 2015.

6. Driver J, Bernard R. Enterprise risk management and its relationship to the Wizard of Oz. *Resources Magazine.* 2013; Summer:37-39.

7. Certified Professional in Healthcare Risk Management (CPHRM). [website] Chicago; IL. American Society of Healthcare Risk Management. http://www.ashrm.org/ashrm/education/programs/cphrm/index.shtml. Accessed October 4, 2015.

8. Robert Wood Johnson Foundation Nursing Research Network. The value of nurse education and residency programs. *Evidence Brief.* May 2011 http://thefutureofnursing.org/sites/default/files/Value%20of%20Nurse%20Education%20and%20Residency%20Programs.pdf. Accessed October 4, 2015.

9. Waterman AD, Garbutt J, Hazel E, et al. The emotional impact of medical errors on practicing physicians in the United States and Canada. *Jt Comm J Qual Patient Saf.* 2007;33(8):467-476.

10. *Stanford Committee for Professional Satisfaction and Support (SCPSS)* [brochure]. Palo Alto, CA: Stanford University Medical Center. Nd. http://med.stanford.edu/gme/current_residents/documents/SCPSSBrochure.pdf. Accessed October 4, 2015.

11. Wallace J, Lemaire J, William G. Physician wellness: a missing quality indicator. *Lancet* 2009;374(9702):1714–1721.

"MAKE NO LITTLE PLANS; THEY HAVE
NO MAGIC TO STIR MEN'S BLOOD AND
PROBABLY THEMSELVES WILL NOT
BE REALIZED. MAKE BIG PLANS; AIM
HIGH IN HOPE AND WORK. "

– Daniel H. Burnham, *Daniel H. Burnham, Architect,*
Planner of Cities

CHAPTER 7

MOBILIZE INNOVATION WITH RICH AND DIVERSE IDEAS

Leilani Schweitzer, Craig Albanese, Matthew Wolden

Advocates and action takers *are needed to take fresh inventive ideas and make them real; without them, the innovators' high aims will go nowhere. Informed and dedicated stakeholders are required to realize successful change. In this chapter, three vignettes show how innovation must occur at all levels of an organization. The vision is driven by engaged individuals and early adopters whose influence is bolstered by their skill, intention and passion for patient safety. The process of change includes everyone in a healthcare organization and, importantly, the patients and their loved ones who experience its care delivery systems.*

ADDRESS AND EASE PROBLEMS

In the film *Field of Dreams*, a pivotal moment occurs when Ray's daughter, Karin, is caught in the middle of a chaotic situation as an argument against Ray's vision ensues. Karin is physically harmed, albeit accidentally, and everyone is forced into action. The crisis takes Doc Graham off the field to help Karin and then opens the eyes of people resistant to the vision and unable to see what is happening around them—the recognition of Ray's vision. Karin recovers. Everyone else is changed.

In *Field of Dreams*, Ray hears a voice telling him to "Ease His Pain" and Ray takes action, not knowing he will ease the pain of many, including himself. In

the context of healthcare, there are many opportunities to prevent and ease the pain of those who feel the impact of unsafe care delivery systems: patients and their families, care providers, and the community. The following series of vignettes show how patient harm—or even near misses—can surface opportunities for system innovation. As they unfold, the vignettes build upon each other to illustrate how events such as these can serve as valuable learning

> It is important to understand the situation from all sides and consider the nurse's experience in the regular course of work.

opportunities that inform improvement and then at the system level--to ease the pain of unsafe care and nontransparent communication. Vignette 1 (right) begins with one version of the story.

Engage Others in Innovation

In assessing the action in Vignette 1, consider the flow of the error from the nurse to the harmed patient and family. It should provide valuable insights on what opportunities exist for improvement. It is important to understand the situation from all sides and consider the nurse's experience in the regular course of work. The nurse received no consideration of how the system and organizational culture

KEY MOTIVATION POINTS:

- Seeing failures and near misses as learning opportunities is vital.

- Implementing change requires partnership and open communication.

- Sharing stories results in engagement and commitment.

A Missed Opportunity

A nursing unit is chaotic. It is understaffed with many high acuity patients. The unit's managers are in meetings at another location. A highly respected and experienced nurse, with multiple patients calling for assistance, rushes to give a medication to a patient. As the nurse is preparing to administer the medication, the amount of the dose seems high. The nurse doesn't feel empowered to question the physician about the order. The physician has a reputation for being reactive and unapproachable with such questions. At the same time, the unit's secretary informs the nurse that two other patients are ringing their call buttons incessantly. The nurse hurries to administer the medication, skipping two identification steps, and thus missing the fact that there's another patient with the same last name on the same unit who was the intended recipient of the medication. The medication error results in serious patient harm.

The nurse is devastated but the unit supervisor asks the nurse to finish the shift because the unit is understaffed. Days go by before the first review of the incident, and weeks pass before further investigation and notice to the organization's patient safety and risk management departments happen. The reviews center on the actions of the nurse, not the state of the environment or the system in which the error occurred. The hospital's patient safety department takes note of the event, but focuses on the fact that the organization's record is still far below that of the national average for the number of adverse drug events.

The patient's family received empathetic and timely support while at the hospital, but was not informed of the facts known about the cause of the harm. Months later the family receives a letter stating that the hospital "takes these events seriously" and has terminated the nurse who caused the harm. The family becomes furious and believes the hospital may be withholding more information as this is the first mention that the harm was preventable. The parents hire a lawyer and are determined to seek the truth and ensure that this will not happen to other patients and families. They vow to sue the hospital. They promise to go to the local press and use social media to reveal the poor and irresponsible care that occurred. An opportunity was missed to create a partnership to engage the family in innovating to improve the care process at the hospital.

failed her as well as the patient and his family. Similarly, consider the trajectory of the incident response and its effect on the family. It is key to see the timely, transparent transfer of information as a restorative element; doing so likely would have eased some of the family's pain. The family was more offended by the hospital's response and poor appreciation of their needs to understand what happened.

Lack of consideration of the perspective of others limits creative problem solving and opportunities to learn from failure.[1] Involving others in the work toward change will result in a more complete understanding of an existing environment to design and embed improvements responding to failure. Doing so requires

seeing a bigger picture and being unwilling to look away from the ugliest and most challenging problems. The best solutions are recognized as part of a whole, not as

> **The inspired patient is the most underutilized and underappreciated resource in healthcare.**

isolated quick fixes. To fully appreciate a problem and devise a solution, all voices and viewpoints must be considered.

It is rare, if not impossible, for an innovation to be flawless upon initial implementation. Engaging early adopters, frontline staff, and customers in iterative improvements leading to a better system—one where

SELECTED READINGS ON PATIENT-CENTEREDNESS

- Berwick DM. What 'patient-centered' should mean: confessions of an extremist. *Health Aff* (Millwood). 2009; 28:w555-w565.

- Gerteis M, Edgman-Levitan S, Daley J, Delbanco TL, eds. *Through the Patient's Eyes: Understanding and Promoting Patient-Centered Care.* San Francisco, CA: Jossey-Bass; 1993.

- Johnson B, Abraham M, Conway J, et al. *Partnering with Patients and Families to Design a Patient- and Family-Centered Health Care System: Recommendations and Promising Practices.* Bethesda, MD: Institute for Family-Centered Care; April 2008.

the creators are also the users—is a key element of success. For example, at the unit described in Vignette 1, the opportunity to learn from the frontline staff and family is lost due to poor response to the incident. To keep from losing this expertise, safety improvement efforts—and early visions of them—need shaping by the various members of the ecosystem. The innovator sparks a chain reaction of change, but the implementers are the ones who carry the idea through, having received and applied the new perspective revealed by that individual. Ray initially hears the voice while in the corn, and does not fully understand what it means or how to respond to what he hears. Ray's dream is realized only when others are enlisted to help, bringing their unique skills and perspectives to the field.

Welcoming the Patient Perspective onto the Field

Patient safety is not a theoretical practice, it is essential for patient and family well-being. For patients and providers, better outcomes are translated as better lives, and those lives are their own.[2] As a whole, patients are no different than the general populace when it comes to embracing change. The inspired patient is the most underutilized and underappreciated resource in healthcare. In any innovative change, including patient engagement, there will be early adopters, and laggards, those too sick and overwhelmed to care about any dream. It is important, therefore, to empower and educate healthcare professionals to recognize the needs and abilities of patients as participants in decision making and improvement work.[3] Partnering with patients by welcoming them onto the field generates clearer communication, as well as greater safety and satisfaction improvements in care delivery systems.

Aim High as a Team

Innovators aim high, however, they cannot have their heads in the clouds and expect change to happen organically. They need people who have their feet on the ground—the early majority—to help realize the dream. Without these implementers who understand what needs to be done and the best way to do it, the translation of the innovator's dream into reality may never materialize. Just as Doc Graham is eager for his chance at bat, without Ray's vision and the support of Shoeless Joe and Terence Mann, Doc Graham will not have the opportunity to play baseball again. Ray, on the other hand, learns from Doc Graham about the importance of commitment to each individual's values and to respect them. In healthcare, partnership, transparency, and engagement between innovators and implementers are of critical importance to ensure successful and sustainable realization of better care. In most cases, these imperatives extend beyond the executive suite, as the absence of perspectives from the frontline staff, patients, and families has a significant impact on the power and success of change.

The hierarchical approach to management, whereby senior executives define priorities and approaches for an entire organization without engaging frontline staff or healthcare consumers, increases risk for everyone. Vignette 1 illustrates the difficulties with this approach including:

- Misunderstanding of the impact of their decisions on daily work demands;
- Resourcing and supervising insufficiencies;
- Over-relying on easy blame and quick fixes to solve safety problems; and most notably,
- Fostering of distrust and minimizing discussion of failure.

Seeking and valuing input from the frontline early majority can expose flaws in the envisioned future state that may go unnoticed by the innovators not participating in day-to-day operations.

Healthcare is now embracing Lean, the management approach widely used in manufacturing to engage the frontline as stewards for improvement. Lean manufacturing principles, developed as part of Toyota's Production System[4], focus on reducing waste and defects to improve quality.

Stanford Children's Health management system uses the Lean principles that echo the Toyota model.[4,5] Following the efforts of Virginia Mason Hospital & Medical Center (Seattle, Washington) Stanford Children's Health uses Lean as a systematic approach to address the multifaceted challenges of safety and efficiency. The key tenets of this system are as follows: quality and safety supersede all other priorities; personnel development and engagement with those on the frontline increase improvement and leadership capacity; collaborative approach strengthens culture, eliminates waste, and improves efficiency. These tenets are achieved through:

- Establishing shared values and vision;
- Building a reliable system to support continuous improvement at every level;
- Treating each problem or defect as an opportunity;

- Supporting transparency;
- Fostering communication; and,
- Focusing on patients.

Staff at Virginia Mason Hospital report feeling both supported in escalating attention to address errors and empowered to help improve processes that prevent recurrence.[6,7] Stanford has also achieved success in applying the Toyota model to care delivery, decreasing preventable harm and also decreasing the frequency of serious safety events (SSEs) and the annual legal payouts associated with them.[8,9]

YOUR VOICE...

VIGNETTE 2:

Small Steps to Broader Commitment

The setting is the same as in Vignette 1: a chaotic understaffed nursing unit. However, rather than ignoring staff resourcing, in this scenario the managers recognize their understaffed unit may represent an at-risk environment for clinical care. The managers quickly assemble with their senior leadership and begin shifting some patients to other units, reprioritize scheduled meetings, and a few of the managers themselves begin caring for patients to mitigate the staffing issue.

In this scenario, when the nurse experiences pressure to rush patient care she responds by invoking the units' escalation system, asking other nurses to help with other patient tasks. Here, medication administration is viewed as a high-risk procedure. To ensure there will be no interruptions, the administering nurse wears a brightly colored vest—a signal to others that she not be interrupted. The established process requires a second nurse to participate in the two-step patient identification procedure. This time the nurse feels safe to question the ordered medication dose because established safety culture allows that anyone can raise a patient safety concern. In such a collaborative safe haven, the physician thanks the nurse for the question and verifies the dose is indeed correct. Unfortunately, the physician believes they are talking about another patient who has the same name. As the nurses begin the identification process, they discover the oversight, halt the medication administration, and so there is no patient harm. The nurse's supervisor discusses the situation with the attending physician and the nurse; together they realize the identification process needs further enhancement. The process improvement is implemented on their unit and on every unit in the medical facility.

BUILD THE FIELD AND THEY WILL COME

In *Field of Dreams*, Ray initially builds the field for Shoeless Joe who then invites others to the field. Good innovators know they need a team to progress. Once the field is built, the influence of early adopters and the early majority drive momentum toward the vision. It takes time and commitment from motivated individuals at all levels of an organization to begin to make a difference. Vignette 2 (left) shows how even incremental system improvements will have a positive effect on the care experience.

See the Team, Not Single Players

Most effective advances in healthcare come from analyzing systems and processes, not from scrutinizing individual people. Focusing on the actions of a single player on a team increases potential for patient harm because it misses the opportunity to address greater system issues. Transparency, enhanced through trust and collaborative team interaction, can be a lens to proactively identify improvement opportunities, as well as potential or existing dangers. It emanates from and encourages a culture that resists blame and seeks collaboration. Failure to be transparent results in missed opportunities to find and fix system failures within an organization.

Transparency and openness in a care team can inspire similar behaviors with patients.[10] Disclosure after an unexpected care outcome encourages partnerships with patients; everyone is on the same team, everyone shares a common goal to understand what happened while

> **Failure to be transparent results in missed opportunities to find and fix system failures within an organization.**

working together to develop improvement strategies. Transparency supports full apology, reconciliation, and healing for everyone involved.

Transparency in communication with patients and their families after an unexpected adverse outcome can maintain trust and promote faster healing by ensuring they have the information needed to understand what led to the event and how it will be avoided for future patients.

Wide Perspectives to Align Vision: Mission Zero at Stanford

Beginning in 2010, a national collaborative of US children's hospitals made eliminating preventable patient harm its top priority.[5] Each participating organization agreed to an All Teach, All Learn model in which best practices would be implemented and as evidence and experience emerged, the information would be shared with the entire collaborative. Many participating organizations have individually branded this priority; at Stanford Children's Health the priority is known as "Mission Zero: Eliminating Preventable Harm." The hospital is working to meet the goal by leveraging its Lean management system to ensure reliable and sustainable compliance with evidence-based standards and improvements in the culture of safety. Success to date has been linked to alignment of priorities and resources and, most importantly, partnership and engagement with the hospital's governing board, leadership team, physicians, frontline staff, as well as patients and their families.

In an effort to ensure Mission Zero remains a top priority, all levels of the organization were aligned and engaged to build consensus. While it was a challenge to get all players on the same field and working toward the same goal, the innovators with the vision understood the need for cross-pollination and collaboration throughout all levels of the organization. An executive patient safety oversight committee provides the backing needed to drive the effort, to maintain focus on engagement throughout the organization, and to ensure adequate resources and support are available to correct identified system weaknesses and remain accountable for such implementation. The aim of Mission Zero aligns with the values structure of the organization; each player who comes to the field desires zero patient harm. With the Mission Zero management system and

governance structure, ideas or dreams can be rapidly deployed throughout the broader community.

COMMUNITY ACCEPTANCE OF THE DREAM

Individual members of the healthcare ecosystem may on any given day recognize the need for change and see multiple improvement opportunities. What inspires some to take action and others to accept the status quo—even after hearing of stories such as that in Vignette 1? Perhaps some have the requisite skills, network, and tools to act and others do not. Some, like Ray, may have the endurance, persistence, and tenacity to see a project through to completion. They may also have Ray's skill to create partnerships and a team by engaging those in the early majority who can collaborate to refine and establish the vision while inviting peers to participate. Others may see an opportunity to improve patient safety, but are too burned out to continue to challenge the status quo, much like Terence Mann before he met up with Ray. It must be acknowledged that change can make things more difficult before it makes them better. Aversion to change may cause resistance to raise its ugly head before it acquiesces to momentum. Ray's story illustrates the value of looking up and refusing to accept the status quo. Despite

TRANSPARENCY PROMOTES HEALING

A CRITICALLY ILL CHILD WAS BEING monitored on the telemetry unit. The frequency of the sounding alarms prevented the child and his mother from getting any sleep. The child's nurse requested the child be moved to the intensive care unit. The nurse's requests for the bed transfer and for assistance in caring for the child were refused. In a compassionate effort to reduce the noise in the room, the nurse silenced the monitor next to the bed. The child's mother thanked her. In giving some quiet to the child and his mother, the nurse inadvertently silenced more than the monitor next to the bed, she silenced the alarms on her pager and at the central unit station. When the child experienced a cardiac event, there was no alarm to notify the nurse or any member of the unit care team. The child died.

The organization thoroughly reviewed the circumstances and discovered a safety issue with the monitoring system that could have an impact on other patients. Rather than focusing on the liability risk to the organization, the focus remained on patient safety. The organization alerted all other hospitals using the same monitors of the event in an effort to prevent harm to other patients. Additionally, the organization continued to share information with the child's family in an effort to express sincere apology and commitment to ensuring such a tragedy did not happen again.

Progress Through Partnership and Respect

The setting is the same chaotic nursing unit. This time, however, the players are aware and acknowledge the realities of healthcare—in this case production pressures in a high acuity, understaffed situation. They know the stakes are high, and are prepared to manage the consequences of their actions.

The nurse feels rushed to administer a questionable dose of medication. The physician in this scenario is not an approachable character. However, the hospital's safety culture provides a safe haven for raising concerns. The nurse phones the ordering physician and together they jointly determine the dosage is correct, but fail to realize each is referring to a different patient with the same name. The nurse skips the two-step identification process and administers the correct drug to the wrong patient. The patient expires.

The event devastates the nurse. It is the first time she has skipped the two-step identification process. The unit supervisor provides emotional support, encourages the nurse to go home, and informs her of the organization's employee counseling program.

The supervisor fills out an incident report and the organization's patient safety team responds within hours. The supervisor notifies a hospital risk manager who ensures a plan to begin disclosure conversations with the family is in place. The risk manager partners with the involved clinicians and the patient safety team to begin gathering facts. A timely root cause analysis to review the event in depth is scheduled. An executive is established as the point of contact with the family to maintain open and honest lines of communication.

The organization's chief executive officer (CEO) contacts the nurse and apologizes for the system failures that placed the nurse under pressure and set the nurse up for failure. In this scenario the organizational reviews focused on What (the process) and Why (the systems)—and not the Who (the nurse) of the event.

The patient's family is given empathetic and timely support while at the hospital and in the following weeks. They are offered a debrief meeting with the CEO. The family is informed of the details of how the death occurred in terms they understand. The family's questions are answered honestly and transparently. The counseling team emphasizes there were system issues that set the nurse up for failure and the hospital takes responsibility for what has occurred. The hospital administrators vow to rectify the issues and make plans to inform the family of the organization's progress on a monthly basis. The family is provided a point of contact, encouraged to call with questions, and offered the opportunity to provide feedback along the way.

After several conversations with hospital administrators and over time, the family's anger and devastation shifts to a desire to partner with the organization through the patient advisory board. The open lines of communication foster trust and a passion for patient safety advocacy. System improvements are timely implemented. The care teams and organization continue to support and augment a culture of safety.

uncertainty and risk, Ray keeps his focus on opportunity and possibility. He recognizes that the success in bringing about his vision of sustaining the field resides in his community's acceptance of the dream.

In building his field, Ray did not clearly understand the outcome and was not fully able to anticipate. He trusted his goal was important, but knew few details. A similar situation arises in healthcare; a collaborative care team prepares for the predictable and the unknown. The team hopes things go well, yet also knows how to react when the situation goes poorly. The team is ready to service the needs of everyone involved: the patient, their

loved ones, the staff and the institution. A culture of safety has prepared them to respond with empathy, support, resolution, and learning to make the best possible improvements.[11] In that spirit, Vignette 3 (left) illustrates how on the new field, the team is realizing improvements and is better prepared to manage system failures that can occur on the path to Mission Zero.

Despite the unfortunate medication delivery system failure anchoring the three vignettes, another system element that aligns with the non-clinical focus of this text was successful. The organization's cultures of

safety and transparency continued to evolve to consider the needs of the individuals involved, future patients and providers. Management and executive leaders were engaged in identifying systemic weaknesses and driving shared accountability for improving them. Most importantly, the

> **Key to inspiring change is not simply creating a vision of an improved future state, but it is garnering agreement on dissatisfaction with the status quo.**

organization embraced the opportunity to partner with the family and respect the patient perspective as a valuable resource in devising solutions to prevent future patient harm.

PARTNERSHIPS ENRICH PROACTIVE SYSTEM IMPROVEMENT

Each of the three vignettes and ensuing discussion illustrate many potential opportunities to promote cultures of safety and transparency. The strategy of incorporating the many existing viewpoints throughout the healthcare ecosystem can proactively guard against the pain the system failure can cause. Human fallibility is real and it occurs. When it does, systems designed to quickly and responsibly manage untoward events must already be in place. The use of open and honest communication is imperative to repair care delivery systems and the trust of everyone involved. Key to inspiring change is not simply creating a vision of an improved future state, but garnering agreement on dissatisfaction with the status quo. Making practical and effective use of the insights and experiences of members throughout the risk and safety ecosystems in healthcare can lead to innovations that can go the distance. Through vision, engagement, multidisciplinary partnership, and effective implementation, the patient safety focus becomes a constant rather than an exception in any interaction or care delivery system.

Proactively preventing harm in medical practices requires keeping patients and the patient experience at the center of the work.[3] All healthcare professionals share in the desire for safe and reliable patient care delivery systems. For clinicians, patient care is their core love of the game. Their ultimate inspiration is to make the lives of

> **On this field everyone owns a stake in care delivery system improvements and has a role as a manager of risk.**

people better—patients, their loved ones, and their communities. Patients want safe, well informed access to the therapies and preventative services they need. They must be informed as partners—even when things go wrong—to understand what happened and begin healing. Clinicians

---

DIGGING DEEPER FOR INSPIRATION:

- Albanese CT, Aaby DR, Platchek TS. *Advanced Lean in Healthcare.* North Charleston, SC: CreateSpace Independent Publishing Platform; 2014.

- Kotter JP, Cohen DS. *The Heart of Change: Real-life Stories of How People Change Their Organizations.* Boston, MA: Harvard Business Press; 2002.

- Pronovost P, Vohr E. *Smart Patients, Smart Hospitals.* New York, NY: Hudson Street Press; 2010.

- Wu AW, ed. *The Value of Close Calls in Improving Patient Safety.* Oakbrook Terrace, IL: Joint Commission Resources; 2011.

should trust their peers and their organizations to create a supportive care environment where fatigue, production pressure, and hierarchy are not allowed to influence the safety of care. On this field everyone owns a stake in care delivery system improvements and has a role as a manager of risk.

References

1. Edmondson AC. Strategies for learning from failure. *Harv Bus Rev*. 2011;89(4):48-55.

2. Leape L, Berwick D, Clancy C, et al; Lucian Leape Institute at the National Patient Safety Foundation. Transforming healthcare: a safety imperative. *Qual Saf Health Care*. 2009;18(6):424-428.

3. Herzer KR Pronovost PJ. Motivating physicians to improve quality: light the intrinsic fire. *Am J Med Qual*. 2014;29(3):451-453.

4. Liker J, *The Toyota Way: 14 Management Principles from the World's Greatest Manufacturer*. McGraw-Hill Education; 2004.

5. Albanese CT, Aaby DR, Platchek TS. *Advanced Lean in Healthcare*. North Charleston, SC: CreateSpace Independent Publishing Platform; 2014.

6. Allen N. Can the Japanese car factory methods that transformed a Seattle hospital work on the NHS? *The Telegraph*. July 3, 2014. [online] http://www.telegraph.co.uk/news/nhs/10940874/Can-the-Japanese-car-factory-methods-that-transformed-a-Seattle-hospital-work-on-the-NHS.html Accessed October 4, 2015.

7. Kenney C. *Transforming Health Care: Virginia Mason Medical Center's Pursuit of the Perfect Patient Experience*. New York, NY: CRC Press; 2010.

8. Blayney DW. Measuring and improving quality of care in an academic medical center. *J Oncol Pract*. 2013;9(3):138-141.

9. Crowe SD, Faulkner B. Lean management system application in creation of a postpartum hemorrhage prevention bundle on postpartum units. *Obstet Gynecol*. 2014;123 Suppl 1:45S.

10. Uhlig PN, Brown J, Nason AK, Camelio A, Kendall E. John M. Eisenberg Patient Safety Awards. System innovation: Concord Hospital. *Jt Comm J Qual Improv*. 2002;28(12):666-672.

11. Conway J, Federico F, Stewart K, Campbell MJ. *Respectful Management of Serious Clinical Adverse Events*. 2nd ed. Cambridge, MA: Institute for Healthcare Improvement; 2011. [online] http://www.ihi.org/resources/pages/ihiwhitepapers/respectfulmanagementseriousclinicalaeswhitepaper.aspx Accessed October 4, 2015.

PART IV: BUILD IT AND THEY WILL COME: STRUCTURE AND STRATEGY FOR LASTING CHANGE

Once a vision is realized, as the new ballfield is built and embraced, the challenge becomes keeping the dream alive. It's imperative to lay the groundwork for sustaining momentum by implementing tools and using strategies the authors suggest—such as decision science, concept communication, and enterprise-wide commitment—to enrich the risk management ecosystem and its role in safe, high quality care. Initiating change is just the beginning. It is important to evolve in ways that matter, to measure and communicate, to test and adjust, and, most importantly, to continually innovate. This is what will sustain the dream.

"THOSE WHO CLING TO THEIR OLD TOOLS AND ALLOW OUR ORGANIZATION TO DISINTEGRATE WILL FIND LITTLE SENSE EITHER IN THE BURNING PRESENT OR THE CHALLENGING FUTURE."

– Donald M. Berwick, *Escape Fire*

CHAPTER 8

A NEW DESIGN, A NEW PARADIGM

Simon Mawer, John Littig, Andrew Azan

 Structural and strategic changes *in the practice of managing risk are necessary to realize the dream of a better healthcare field. Considering first how resources, such as time, are allocated will allow more space in a risk management program to increase focus on the proactive management of risk. This will enable value-driven initiatives to take flight. Risk management professionals need key process tools to take their programs to the next level—the best-practice level. These tools include decision science and design thinking.*

ALLOCATE RESOURCES TO STRUCTURE AND SUPPORT INNOVATION

Visionary risk management professionals can see endless stepping stones toward improvement in healthcare ecosystems. Some of these opportunities need immediate attention to mitigate impact from realized risk; others jump and scream for attention, but in reality less is at stake. Allocating risk resources, including time, requires prioritization. Managers of risk should think in this way when they plan how to apportion their time: focus on high value, high return activities first. They need to continually make decisions about how to invest their resources based on the expected value that alternate investment opportunities may bring to their risk programs. For example, at the beginning of *Field of Dreams*, it didn't make sense for Ray to invest much in a parking lot for those coming to the new ballfield—at that point, the field was still a dream. Yet, at the end of the film, the line of cars stretching across Iowa corn country then represented a business opportunity—and increased liability. For example, it is conceivable Ray might eventually come to care a bit more about parking and derive a bit of revenue from it. The key to risk management is not knowing what will happen, but being prepared to manage uncertainty.

In his famous commentaries on the nature of risk and uncertainty, *Blackswan*

> ## KEY MOTIVATION POINTS:
>
> - **Time is a valuable resource. Allocate it wisely to get the most out of proactive efforts.**
> - **Value is the new risk management mindset.**
> - **Decision and design tools help build a value driven risk management program.**
> - **Captives can be a springboard for supporting a new vision for managing risk.**

and *Antifragile*, Nassim Taleb makes an impassioned case for understanding that the nature of the world is not a smooth upward slope, but rather a smooth slope for a time and then a shock—be it war, natural disaster, or economic depression. To be sure, *something* will happen next.[1,2] Healthcare risk and medical malpractice claims follow a similar pattern: long quiet periods of normal practice followed by extreme shock losses (significant losses that have an impact on insurance practices). Managing variation during quiet periods is of low, long-term utility and may lend itself to overconfidence in the ability to manage risk. Planning and preparing for shock losses, on the other hand, can be the difference between continued existence and bankruptcy.

TIME IS A MANAGEABLE RESOURCE: INVEST WISELY

The amount of resources at a risk manager's discretion to use to pursue a vision of improvement will be informed by many factors outside their control, including historical budgets, administrative understanding of the vision, and current economic realities of the healthcare system. Every day, managers of risk make value judgments of where and how to deploy resources—not the least of which is time. In fact, time is a very important part of this equation: how many hours do staff invest in the status quo versus new approaches, and in what order of priority?

Risk managers have a limited amount of time—approximately 2,000 hours per year. An effective first step for managing their time is to keep track of it. Similar to the concept of billable hours, risk management departments can quantify the amount of time spent on day-to-day risk management activities by client or departments, project work, and education programs.[3] Time investment data can help reveal the status quo. It can provide an overall picture of where time resources are being spent, and thereby reveal opportunities for making value-driven allocation decisions towards building the field. A good place to start to understand how time and energy can be

THE FUTURE IS UNDER NO OBLIGATION TO ACT LIKE THE PAST

A FAMOUS PARABLE of a turkey serves as a insightful illustration to encourage more robust understanding of future risk as it relates to the past. Every day the farmer comes and feeds the turkey. Day after day, week after week, and month after month the turkey comfortably comes to believe the farmer is benevolent and wants nothing more than the turkey to be happy, healthy, and fat—until Thanksgiving, that is, when it is no longer a very good idea to trust the farmer.[1] By prioritizing opportunities in terms of which are the easiest, loudest, or by relying on simply doing what has always been done, risk managers can be in jeopardy of becoming turkeys themselves.

redirected to pursue a goal is to track time allocation for one month. Compare the time investment to strategic goals and then make considered, value-driven decisions to narrow the gap.

 In the film *Field of Dreams*, Ray reallocates his time and makes space to enable his dream to materialize, and starts by plowing under a section of nearly mature corn. Consider this: what if he had waited a month longer to harvest the corn and build the field then? Shoeless Joe Jackson hadn't had his pain eased in upwards of 60 years; yet a sense of urgency and passion made Ray proceed when patience may have served him financially. The lesson here is to optimize and capture the maximum value and bring stakeholders along for the journey. Risk management professionals will realize success in their efforts through partnership, patience and strategic thinking.

Time Management Strategies

A key strategy for effective time allocation for risk management professionals is training leaders throughout the enterprise to, as appropriate, manage risks within their respective areas. A service mentality is both a blessing and a curse for the effective risk manager. The sacred cow of service provision to all perpetuates an organization-wide misunderstanding of the most effective role of risk management.

To successfully navigate disparate challenges while pursuing the vision of improvement requires a firm understanding of the boundaries of professional risk management responsibilities and where efforts are best spent.

Part of building the field is engaging others in education about strategies for managing potential or perceived risk within their respective areas. Empower others as managers of risk. This will further the goal of an enterprise risk management model by establishing partnerships and accountability for appropriate problem-solving. The strategy also clarifies and

> **Risk management professionals will realize success in their efforts through partnership, patience and strategic thinking.**

standardizes work within the risk management program itself. Rather than the individualized hacking approach that Ray embraced, building a new field in healthcare requires incremental steps, small wins, cross-pollination, and collective buy-in with a focus on a larger goal supporting a greater good. Risk management leaders must be prepared to articulate a vision to early adopters, and then work with them to develop the strategy to get there. As often and appropriately as possible, leaders must be willing to tell the story—the one that illuminates the need for change—in order to effectively gain leverage and optimize support from early adopters and key stakeholders.[4,5]

ONE OF THE BASIC TENANTS of Lean methodology is standardization of work. A simple idea with powerful implications for risk management programs, standardization of work enables the delegation of duties and diffusion of responsibility to the appropriate level and no higher.

For example, consider that the US Navy teaches rotating men and women as young as 18 years old to maintain and fly jets, freeing senior officers to concern themselves with the mission at hand. While the US Navy sets a very high bar for delegation via processes, redundancies, and training, risk management programs can use many of the same techniques to similarly reallocate time to proactive strategy while ensuring that day-to-day operations continue.

A NEW MINDSET CENTERED ON CREATING VALUE

It is hard to imagine a time when the challenges we faced so vastly exceeded the creative resources we have brought to bear on them.

— Tim Brown, *Change…by Design*

In *Field of Dreams*, Ray Kinsella plows down a large, financially viable part of his family's cornfield to build a baseball diamond in pursuit of a bold personal vision. He took apart something that appeared to be working and built something else that, at first appearance, seemed to not work at all. Even though Ray experienced a good outcome, would a more collaborative approach have yielded an even better result? Throughout healthcare risk and safety ecosystems, a bold vision needs to be embraced by all: to completely eliminate preventable harm. To realize the vision, small, daily, incremental improvements can move the bar forward. Innovations

> … a bold vision needs to be embraced by all: to completely eliminate preventable harm.

are also necessary to rethink, redesign and transform ineffective and unsafe healthcare delivery systems. The field is ripe for disruption, and that will require making room for something new.

Innovative disruptions in traditional care practices can create feelings of unease by seeming to break something that relatively works in order to build something that may not. For the healthcare industry, this may represent a shift from disease and injury management to preventative population health and wellness maintenance. Disruptive innovation may mean rethinking how the operating room functions, or dismantling traditional hierarchies.

In the management of healthcare risk, progressive disruption can better prepare everyone to be managers of risk. The historical risk management perspective looks only to protect value—to keep the farm producing what it has always produced. For risk management professionals, this shift means an evolution away from a traditional value protection orientation and a practice that focuses on downside clinical risks in discrete silos. In place of the protectionist focus, a concern for enterprise-wide, existing and emerging risks and unrealized upside value opportunities—a new, enterprise-wide value-creating mindset—takes hold.[6] The mindset helps these professionals see the current field and what the field could be. They can drop their old tools entirely, or enhance the use of tried and true favorites to arrive at new ways of doing things in an environment they help create. With a holistic enterprise-oriented perspective, they are able to make decisions not just on limiting downside losses, but also with value-creation considerations.

A late adopter may be uncomfortable with the idea that value creation should be a part of their job description. To some, the shift may sound as illogical as a farmer deciding that part of his job is to build a baseball field. In order to achieve audacious goals for quality and safety improvement, a new mindset and philosophy are required to establish risk management professionals as stewards of enterprise value. Along with the new mindset, they will also need new tools to effectively communicate the vision to leadership across the enterprise.

DROPPING OLD TOOLS TO CREATE OPPORTUNITIES TO DESIGN NEW ONES

 It is tempting to think the ends justified the means for Ray, but the complexity, stakes, and range of stakeholders in healthcare will require a comprehensive articulation of value of a proposed vision. It is ill advised to impulsively mow down the corn. While Ray's wife, Annie, gives unquestioning acceptance to her husband's vision, that kind of unconditional support is not likely to be shared by senior executives. Compelling explanations of the value to be realized, broad consensus across multiple disciplines, and expert implementation that can show demonstrable returns on investment over time are necessary.

Naturally, such an approach will augment the kinds of activities currently viewed as valuable investments of time and resources. Risk registries, heat maps, and the like are trusted tools for highlighting the greatest loss drivers by frequency and severity. But in order to achieve clarity regarding which risk mitigation efforts will result in the greatest value back to the organization, risk management programs need something more.

The standard downside focused risk management processes and tools need to be augmented, buttressed, and supplemented with the complementary and overlapping mindsets, processes, and tools of decision quality, decision analysis, and design thinking:

- **DECISION QUALITY:** A framework for getting to the right decision via decision analysis and other process tools.
- **DECISION ANALYSIS:** A social-technical discipline that quantifies and helps explain the value of one course of action over the other.

- **DESIGN THINKING:** A generative, ethnographic process for coming up with innovative alternatives and solutions that meet the real needs of the intended end users.

These are all helpful tools risk management professionals can use as the engine room, so to speak, for tackling the biggest challenges they face. It can be helpful to discuss each separately by reference to the most unique contributions they bring to the table to tackle the biggest risk management challenges.

Decision Quality

Decision quality is a framework for understanding and communicating the essential elements that afford good decision making about risk investments. It provides healthcare professionals with a range of tools for ensuring that decisions are the best they can possibly be, and for anticipating the potential ways best efforts can come undone. Central to decision quality is the understanding that there is an important distinction between decisions and outcomes. Often, a decision is erroneously defined as being either good or bad by the quality of the outcome. However, when dealing with upside and downside risk and future uncertainties, it is quite possible to have a good decision

Table 8.1: **Decision/Outcome Matrix for Ray's Innovation**		
	GOOD OUTCOME	**BAD OUTCOME**
GOOD DECISION	DESERVED SUCCESS: Harvested cornfield, sold at high prices, family flourishes	BAD BREAK: Harvested cornfield, poor economy, poor income, family scrapes by
BAD DECISION	LUCK: Plow down cornfield to build baseball field, Shoeless Joe Jackson arrives, draws huge crowd, family flourishes	POETIC JUSTICE: Plow down cornfield to build baseball field, nothing happens, family loses farm

Inspired by Russo and Schoemaker, *Winning Decisions.*[7]

result in a bad outcome, and a bad decision work out much better than expected. Table 8.1 demonstrates the Decision/Outcome Matrix for Ray's situation.

Considering Ray's decision to plow down his cornfield given the information he had at the time, how should his decision be classified? A good decision with a good outcome, or something else?

Decision quality principles maintain that the quality of a decision should be judged by the process used to arrive at that decision given the alternatives, information, and preferences known at the time the decision is made, and not by the outcome.[8] The decision quality chain, a useful tool building off the work of David and James Matheson

to understand the essential elements required to make a high quality decision, requires six elements—frame, alternatives, information, values, reasoning, and commitment—for a high quality decision.[9] In such a framework, a decision is only as good as its weakest dimension, and a crack in the process at any point will result in falling into the valley of decision failure.

Using the elements of decision quality (Figure 8.1), consider Ray's decision making process and whether it could have been aided by coming up with well-described answers to the following:

- **FRAME:** Clarifying what needs to be decided and the appropriate frame for the opportunity. Asking what can be created and what needs to be decided, when and by whom?

- **ALTERNATIVES:** Developing a range of high quality, significantly different yet doable alternatives. Determining what are the various ways in which this decision can be made? Are there alternatives left unappreciated?
- **INFORMATION:** Defining what needs to be known to make a decision. Using meaningful, trustworthy, reliable data and evidence to understand the past. Drawing from what is known to make unbiased judgements and high-quality probability assessments about the present and future.
- **VALUES:** Clarifying the values and preferences bearing on the decision: what is the purpose? What is the risk appetite? Is the decision consistent with the organization's mission, values, and culture? What consequences of the decision are cause for concern? What outcomes are of interest?
- **REASONING:** Using logical and sound reasoning to consider the hard and soft factors making an impact on the value of the alternative(s) been considered.
- **COMMITMENT:** Determining the intention to act. Demonstrating commitment to follow through organizational buy-in and allocation of sufficient resources to ensure

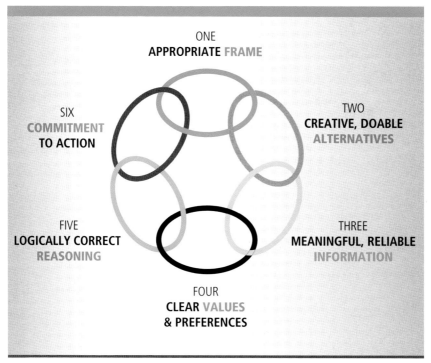

ONE
APPROPRIATE FRAME

SIX
**COMMITMENT
TO ACTION**

TWO
**CREATIVE, DOABLE
ALTERNATIVES**

FIVE
**LOGICALLY CORRECT
REASONING**

THREE
**MEANINGFUL, RELIABLE
INFORMATION**

FOUR
**CLEAR VALUES
& PREFERENCES**

Figure 8.1: **Decision Quality Chain**
Inspired by Matheson and Matheson, *The Smart Organization*.[9]

appropriate access to the time, effort, money and planning needed to support effective implementation.

As the early majority considers changing their framework and approach to risk, they can benefit from looking inside first by analyzing their own history. Thinking through experiences with organizational initiatives, how many have rated high in quality on every dimension, but have failed because:

- They don't fully understand the true nature or complexity of the problem.
- They chose an alternative in conflict or at cross-purpose with the values or preferences of the organization or a key stakeholder.
- They miss an alternative that was not considered as part of the process.
- They do not have or do not seek to find a key piece of available information.
- They misinterpret the values or preferences of the environment in which the decision was going to live.
- They incorrectly quantify the potential costs and benefits of the decision.
- They lack the requisite ongoing commitment to allocate sufficient resources to ensure successful implementation.

YOUR VOICE...

Ray had a high commitment to implementation, but he lacked deep understanding of the opportunity he was seeking to launch. He did not consider alternatives such as first harvesting his corn and then building the ballfield, nor did he seek additional information before moving forward. Lastly, hearing a voice in the night and seeing a vision of a baseball field among the corn does not qualify as logical reasoning. In order to achieve healthcare's field of dreams, risk management professionals will need to make high quality decisions about where to spend time and resources. Decision quality can provide a robust framework for working through those decisions so as to avoid many of the common pitfalls. It is time to aim for deserved success and not rely on luck alone.

Decision Analysis

At any given moment, in any given week, risk managers are presented with many different opportunities to improve patient safety, promote clinical effectiveness, and reduce or eliminate unintended harm. But which activities will deliver the most value to the organization?

Decision analysis is a social-technical discipline that has become the standard method in many industries for producing clarity about the best choice to make in the face of an uncertain and dynamic environment.[10] Through a range of quantitative and qualitative tools and processes, decision analysis enables professionals to consider and understand all of the upside and downside risks, actions and uncertainties that bear on a decision. In turn, this empowers leaders to identify and choose to implement those interventions that have the highest potential to deliver the greatest value back to the institution.

Luckily for Ray, as time went on, his family and friends came on board as they began to see the evidence resulting from the realization of his vision. In healthcare, seldom is there such a long rope to potentially bankrupt the family farm in pursuit of a blurry vision. Being able to describe the vision and present a robust business case for why a new direction makes sense are essential, and decision analysis provides practical tools to those ends.

Design Thinking

If decision quality is the overarching framework for getting to the right choice via decision analysis and other complementary process tools, design thinking is one of the most valuable models risk managers should draw from to generate high quality ideas and alternatives. Design thinking is an approach to innovation and problem solving that makes practical and effective use of the tools and mindsets designers traditionally use to address challenges outside of the ordinary realm of design. It is an approach to tackling new challenges that places the explicit and latent needs of the intended end user as paramount.[11]

Healthcare leaders have most likely seen projects fail because selected tactics didn't meet the needs for which the solution was developed to address. Design thinking's great strength is its focus on ensuring that the created product, service, or strategy meets the needs of the end users—in healthcare, the patients and the clinicians. It employs a structured process and a range of tools that guide decision makers through fostering deep empathy with the end users for which the solution is being designed. Tactics such as immersion, observation and open-ended interviews build empathy with end users and understanding of the problem space. Synthesis methods help define opportunity areas. Brainstorming and prototyping bring solutions to life.[12] Finally, through rapid experiments with end users, creative and effective strategies are collaboratively refined and launched.[12]

Design thinking can be viewed as a sort of dance forward and backward, and throughout three different spaces of inspiration, ideation, and implementation.[12] For example:

- **INSPIRATION:** Where the designer seeks to understand the problem or opportunity that motivates the creative process of solution finding.
- **IDEATION:** Where new ideas are generated, evaluated, and prototyped.
- **IMPLEMENTATION:** Where the idea is launched into the real world.[13]

Each endeavor begins with an investigation into end user's behaviors and experiences which then reveals needs, desires, and new ways of meeting both. Cross-disciplinary tools and methods are used to visualize, evaluate, and refine opportunities for innovation, design, and development. These include:

- Illuminating and confirming why people behave the way they do—not just by asking them, but by paying attention to what they do and what they believe.
- Helping stakeholders collaboratively envision the future.
- Understanding the interplay among constituents throughout a system.
- Introducing potential design solutions in low-cost, low-risk ways.

- Iterating quickly to test different solutions, revise them based on user feedback, and ultimately refine the product or experience.
- Creating ways to effectively and efficiently spread and scale solutions.

Although there is some overlap between the design thinking process and the decision quality framework, both disciplines explore a problem from different, but complementary perspectives. Pairing them together leverages the strengths of each approach to identifying, prioritizing, and generating high quality, human-centered solutions to the most pressing issues facing both patients and providers.

Risk management must strive to make the highest quality decisions about improving the delivery of care. The effort will involve using the best tools available to identify the areas of greatest loss and opportunity in the organization; design high quality, human-centered solutions in close consultation with patient and provider end users; analyze those solutions to determine which ones will have the greatest positive impact on the institution; and finally, present that information in such a way so as to achieve stakeholder support and buy-in. Decision quality, decision analysis,

and design thinking all provide valuable, complementary mindsets, tools, and processes for helping risk management programs become agents of positive change. They are essential to achieving the dream.

DRAWING SUPPORT FROM THE ECOSYSTEM

The ability to obtain funding for various loss mitigation or prevention projects is a constant challenge for risk management programs. Often, the operating budget process is poorly equipped to consider the value protection and value creation of potential risk management efforts. Return on investment calculations for risk management can be difficult to quantify without the right tools and involves proving the negative. Fortunately, the operating budget isn't the only place to look for support; many healthcare organizations have self-insurance vehicles in place to fund non-catastrophic medical malpractice losses. Such vehicles can be as simple as a balance sheet accrual or as complicated as an offshore captive insurer. They are usually governed by leadership of the organization and are charged with limiting the impact of losses on the operating results of the company. The self-insurance vehicle has the capital and the political power to support risk management efforts in so far as they are intended to prevent and reduce losses for which the self-insurer is responsible. Risk management programs should use these vehicles as kindling for their vision. Beyond the operating budget and self-insurance vehicle, risk management programs can also look to their insurers and/or reinsurers for support. These partners are aligned with risk management in a desire to prevent and mitigate losses; they're often willing to offer grants, premium discounts, or premium paybacks based on achieving specific goals.

Innovators get some leeway in the beginning, however, at some point they need the metrics and social structure to sustain the vision. Ray didn't mow down all of his corn, and the players all retreat to what is left standing when the game is

> **Ray didn't mow down all of his corn, and the players all retreat to what is left standing when the game is done. If risk management programs don't continue to do the basics well, they could still miss the chance to improve and create value from their services.**

done. If risk management programs don't continue to do the basics well, they could still miss the chance to improve and create value from their services. Building a new field will give risk management programs a chance to thrive.

DIGGING DEEPER FOR INSPIRATION:

- Brown T. *Change by Design: How Design Thinking Transforms Organizations and Inspires Innovation.* New York, NY: HarperCollins Publishers; 2009.

- Hubbard DW. *The Failure of Risk Management: Why It's Broken and How to Fix It.* Hoboken, NJ: Wiley; 2009.

- Matheson D, Matheson JE. *The Smart Organization: Creating Value Through Strategic R&D.* Boston, MA: Harvard Business School Press; 1998.

References

1. Taleb NN. *The Black Swan: The Impact of the Highly Improbable.* New York, NY: Random House; 2007.

2. Taleb NN. *Antifragile: Things That Gain From Disorder.* New York, NY: Random House; 2012.

3. ECRI Institute. Strategies to prove risk management = value. *Risk Manage Rep.* 2011;30(3):1,4-9.

4. Denning S. Telling tales. *Harv Bus Rev.* 2004;82(5):122-129, 152.

5. Institute for Safe Medication Practices. Telling true stories is an ISMP hallmark: here's why you should tell stories, too. *ISMP Medication Safety Alert! Acute Care Edition.* September 8, 2011;16:1-3. http://www.ismp.org/newsletters/acutecare/showarticle.aspx?id=4 Accessed October 4, 2015.

6. Celona J, Driver J, Hall E. Value-driven ERM: making ERM an engine for simultaneous value creation and value protection. *J Healthc Risk Manage.* 2011;30(4):15-33.

7. Russo JE, Schoemaker PJH. *Winning Decisions: Getting It Right the First Time.* NewYork, NY: Doubleday; 2002.

8. McNamee P. Celona J. *Decision Analysis with Supertree: Instructor's Manual,* 2nd ed. South San Francisco, CA: The Scientific Press; 1991.

9. Matheson D, Matheson JE. *The Smart Organization: Creating Value Through Strategic R&D.* Boston, MA: Harvard Business School Press; 1998.

10. Parenell GS, Bresnick TA, Tani SN, Johnson ER. *Handbook of Decision Analysis.* Hoboken, NJ: John Wiley & Sons, Inc; 2013.

11. Walters H. "Design Thinking" isn't a miracle cure, but here's how it helps. *Fast Company Design.* March 24, 2011. [online] http://www.fastcodesign.com/1663480/design-thinking-isnt-a-miracle-cure-but-heres-how-it-helps Accessed October 4, 2015.

12. Brown T. Design thinking. *Harv Bus Rev.* 2008;86(6):84-92.

13. Brown T. *Change by Design: How Design Thinking Transforms Organizations and Inspires Innovation.* New York, NY: HarperCollins Publishers; 2009.

"THE PERSON WHO SAYS IT CANNOT
BE DONE SHOULD NOT INTERRUPT
THE PERSON DOING IT."

– Chinese Proverb

CHAPTER 9

ENABLE OTHERS TO EMBRACE THE DREAM

Matthew Wolden, Dana Welle

Innovators and leaders—*while challenged by individuals who don't embrace their dreams—cannot let them derail progress. To best address this reality, innovators must gain the attention of those who are slow to take up a change: the late majority. The late majority have perceptions that affect their willingness to meaningfully participate in implementing new ideas. Communication and executive actions that demonstrate the evidence, goals, impact, and value of change can help those in the late majority to align with the innovator's vision and contribute their knowledge to improving patient safety and quality.*

CHALLENGE OF THE LATE MAJORITY

According to diffusion researchers, individuals can be classified based on their propensity to adopt a specific innovation.[1,2] Each type of individual has his or her own personality based on their acceptance of new ideas. Therefore, strategies for moving innovation forward will succeed only if presented and packaged to meet the specific needs of each set.[1] Late adopters—whether Rogers' late majority or laggards—are conventional individuals who shy away from risk and are most comfortable living with what they know. They are most apt to operate under the status quo. Late majority adopters can interrupt progress and stall momentum. They can be motivated by the fear of being ostracized, so they will conform to mainstream standards but are often influenced by the fears and opinions of laggards.[3]

The effective use and influence of true early adopters, as well as the support of both formal and informal organizational networks, are central to the diffusion of innovation.[4] It is imperative that organizations identify individuals who can serve as role models or champions who can persuade peers to accept new ideas. Change capacity will increase as organizations find champions who cover several key sectors, such as clinicians, administrators, legal partners, and staff.

In healthcare, patient safety and quality outcomes will advance only when those in the traditional silos are released and brought together, and are encouraged to understand each stakeholder's interest in the common goal through collaboration and partnership initiatives.

Acceptance of innovation can be viewed on a bell-shaped continuum. (See Figure P.1, page 6) Rather than concentrating on persuading people to change, diffusion focuses on the representation of the new concept or path to be taken so it is tailored to meet the needs of the individual to motivate them to come on board.[3] Some experts label the difference between innovators and the late majority as a chasm.[5] However, Everett Rogers' diffusion

KEY MOTIVATION POINTS:

- Seeing resistance to innovation through the eyes of others sparks understanding.

- Preventing tragedy and harm can generate buy-in and engagement.

- Living and breathing in support of the vision moves others to embrace the dream.

ADOPTING CHANGE:

A SIMPLE EXAMPLE of the variety of acceptance can be illustrated in the way individuals adapt to the increasing changes in technology. There are those who embrace the new technology as quickly as it is developed. They are the ones who need the latest updated gadget—a smart phone, for instance—right now and don't care if their phone contract won't allow for an upgrade, they will happily pay full price for the new device. In contrast, others will wait until the second version appears on the market, has had a test run, maybe had an opportunity to have the bugs worked out, before upgrading. Still others will go so far as to let their phone upgrade lapse, taking the time to observe and examine the newest technology to determine if they indeed trust it.

of innovation theory rejects the idea of a chasm and instead proposes individuals form more of a continuum.[3] This unique approach requires leaders to understand what is important to each individual across the innovation acceptance spectrum and to tailor the significance of the new idea to meet the needs of the individual. For the more risk averse late majority, it is valuable to explore methods that recognize and address fear and resistance. The process starts with getting their attention and feedback toward gaining their buy-in on the change. Once committed, innovators, early adopters, and the early majority can work together to devise ways to support the individuals through the change process.

Given the over-abundance of information and demands on healthcare professionals,

getting their attention is more difficult than might be imagined. It has been said that Winston Churchill espouses leaders should "Never let a good crisis go to waste"[6]—it's an attitude that rather accurately reflects how healthcare has traditionally managed risk and patient safety. In today's culture of fear-based, if-it-bleeds-it-leads media programming, tragedy is apt to get people's attention. But waiting for a tragedy to motivate action is reactive and careless.

In *Field of Dreams*, it is a potential crisis that brings the primary late majority character, Mark, to understand the restorative significance of Ray replacing his cornfield with a ballfield. Initially, Mark doubts Ray's vision can be successful and believes pursuing the aspiration will cost

Ray his farm. The disagreement catches Ray's daughter, Karin, in the middle of the chaos and she is inadvertently harmed. When Doc Graham, a key player, comes to the aid of the injured Karin, his actions open Mark's eyes to what Ray is trying to accomplish. Once Mark buys in to Ray's goal, Mark is committed to it and wants to support it. In healthcare, the illustration translates to a desired experience of increased participation and accountability for patient safety. An engaged workforce with a shared vision is essential to bringing late adopters on board and expanding these effort to sustain the goal. Once they have accepted and understand the value of the change, the skills of late adopters can be applied to support success.

In order to sustain an innovation's implementation, it is imperative to understand how the innovation will be received by those upon whom it will have an impact. It is also important to realize a new way of doing something does not have to be a dramatic, disruptive change; continuous improvements over time can also result in success, although perhaps less obviously. Incremental change mirrors the slow evolution of late adopter beliefs and values, which can be an advantage; when pointed out to the late adopter, it can highlight the importance of accepting a different approach, process or role.[7]

PERCEPTION IS NINE-TENTHS REALITY: FRAME IT WITH CARE

Healthcare organizations have a complex infrastructure—comprised of various stakeholders with different goals— that influences the success of strategic initiatives. In order for an organization to be sustainable and thrive, it must embrace the creation and adaptation of new ideas from all stakeholders. To do that, it must coalesce around a common mission to further unite efforts. Often the focus of patient safety and improved care outcomes is a theme all individuals can appreciate and one that can unify a complex organization. Successful roll out of change in healthcare and other settings requires frameworks that allow cyclical processing. Similar to managing risk in an enterprise encompassing framework such as ERM, improved clinical effectiveness efforts must also be sharply defined and iterative. The ability to frame and manage varying influences related to individual perception and leadership support of change are important focal points.[8] Primary influences that affect the success of change implementation include:

- **EVIDENCE:** When staff believes that the organization should accept the status quo as clinically effective enough, they will be less inclined to be in favor of redesign, reinvention or restructuring. The discrepancy in what is and what should be—that is, relative advantage—

is more easily communicated if quantified or illustrated with evidence. Evidence provides concrete terms that demonstrate, prove, document, and quantify the need for change implementation.[1] Relative advantage is the degree to which change is perceived as being better than the current status quo. The greater the perceived relative advantage of an innovation, such as economic, social recognition, convenience, or satisfaction, the more rapid the rate of adoption.[1,8] For late adopters, it is imperative to understand their personal motivations; the more successful leaders and executives are at aligning goals of the innovation with goals of the individual, the faster the adoption.

- **DEMONSTRATION:** To further encourage late adaptors, it is valuable to demonstrate the change in the environment where it will occur; that it is doable and will work. Similarly, the perception that the change will benefit the adopter in a way that is important to them will improve acceptance of the idea.[8] Benefit or value can be demonstrated by internal or external sources. Internal benefits that can shift the adopter's perception include personal satisfaction, increased support for professional education, and team learning opportunities. External benefits include individual recognition, job security, and realized process improvements.[8]

- **EXECUTIVE SUPPORT:** Support from C-suite and board members is a key component of any change effort.[9,10] When leaders are implementing fresh strategies and tactics, actions speak louder than words.[11] Late adopters will be more

EXPERIENCE FROM THE FIELD:

AS PART OF THE PATIENT SAFETY transformation and focus on eliminating preventable harm at Lucile Packard Children's Hospital Stanford, a deliberate effort is made to link evidence-based processes with their outcomes. One example of this is how the hospital monitors compliance with an evidence-based protocol for preventing central-line associated blood stream infection. Data gathered in review of individual outcomes related to central-line placement quantifies a rate of compliance with the evidence-based protocol. The measurement illuminates cause and effect for staff by demonstrating how individual actions can prevent or contribute to patient harm and encourages consideration for individual accountability.

likely to accept creative modifications if they see those managing the changes also living by the new rules.

- **GOAL RELEVANCE:** Innovative ideas that are compatible with values, norms, or practices will be more readily and rapidly adopted than ideas that are not.[1] In the film, the connection of Annie's philosophies to the freedom of the 1960s, Terence Mann's articulation of those values, and the importance of freedom to follow a different path all contributed to her acceptance of Ray's goals to build a ballfield and bring people to it. The benefits of a proposed innovation should be clearly outlined to all affected stakeholders with the aim of enhancing their motivation to support it.[8] Customizing the education and translating how personal behaviors will affect the system can motivate and inspire desire to participate in the implementation of something new.

- **PURPOSEFUL COMMUNICATION:** It is important to describe how change is intended to address a current problem and improve the system for all involved. Purposeful communication enhances teamwork, positive relationship building, and the sharing of ideas.[8] Chapter 7 of this book discusses the organizational commitment to the Mission Zero culture change at Lucile Packard Children's Hospital Stanford, and is one example of incorporating purposeful communication in daily practice. The organization implemented a series of cultural interventions developed by Healthcare Performance Improvement (HPI) that built on the use of standard communication tools for use in more challenging areas of daily practice, such as problem solving, error reporting and leadership driven system improvement.

- **RELATABILITY:** Amending the change initiative message to the acceptance style of the adopter improves relatability and goal alignment. Then, demonstrating how the adopter can build on inherent strengths to perform tasks chosen in consideration of alignment with those strengths will increase the uptake of change. New ideas that are simple to understand are adopted more rapidly than ideas that require the individual to develop new skills and understandings.[8,12] As the results of the innovation become more apparent, the more likely uncertainty and rejection of the change will decrease. Visibility of value also encourages collegial discussion and information sharing between the adopters and others involved in change implementation.[1]

COMMITMENT TO HOSPITAL-ACQUIRED INFECTION REDUCTION: AN EXAMPLE

HOSPITAL-ACQUIRED INFECTIONS (HAI) are a pervasive healthcare problem that is largely dependent on human behavior and compliance with evidence-based standards. In 1976, the Joint Commission (then called the Joint Commission on Accreditation of Healthcare Organizations, or JCAHO) made infection control programs mandatory; hospitals were required to have them in place in order to receive hospital accreditation.[13] Over the course of the next several decades, hospitals established infection control programs and began measuring and reporting rates of infection against benchmarks.[13] Lucile Packard Children's Hospital Stanford, for instance, consistently performs better than the many national targets, but in most cases the rate is still not zero, which means that within the rate are actual patients whose experiences inspire the hospital staff to work harder at getting to a zero rate. A critical tipping point occurred when the organization began shifting internal reporting of HAI events from rates with benchmarks to absolute numbers representing individual patients. The shift was an illustration of the first time the dream of innovators and the work of the early adopters began to build momentum and an early majority was realized.

As a culture of safety becomes more evident and established in an organization, it is more difficult for laggards to continue to resist change—and even if the laggards remain disinclined to participate, they may still benefit from the change. In the film, when Ray plowed up his cornfield, his community thought him to be crazy, and yet ultimately Ray succeeded. Despite the community's reluctance to accept his ideas, it will likely benefit from what Ray created and over time, the community's perception may change. Through perseverance and consideration of their personal ability to contribute to improvement efforts, it is possible to continue to attract and engage late adopters.

Multidisciplinary and transparent problem analysis support pointed data and information sharing strategies. When a safety event is detected, it is thoroughly reviewed to discover root causes, and the subsequent improvements are broadly, frequently, and transparently shared among the involved healthcare players. Identifying individuals who are involved in safety events and who are willing to openly share their stories without fear of retribution and with the full support of the leadership team has been a most powerful method of shifting the culture of blame to a culture of safety.

BUILDING THE PLACE FOR APPROVAL OF THE FIELD

Across healthcare risk and safety ecosystems, innovative change must become part of the organizational culture. Lucile Packard Children's Hospital Stanford began its Lean journey in 2010, and over the course of the next several years, it designed and operationalized a daily management system across the organization. One of the primary components of the system is the development and implementation of established practice for preventing hospital-acquired conditions. The agreed upon tactics are supported by tiered daily huddles, standard visual management, and process monitoring that engages the frontline team and management. Even individuals who resisted contributing to the reservoir of knowledge are empowered to benefit from it. Once they do, it is likely they'll be more apt to participate.

Acceptance of new ideas and tactics involves managing some individual comfort levels with change and accountability. Each person requires targeted encouragement

DIGGING DEEPER FOR INSPIRATION:

- Berwick DM. Disseminating innovations in health care. *JAMA*. 2003;289(15):1969-1975.

- Bunting RF Jr. Healthcare innovation barriers: results of a survey of certified professional healthcare risk managers. *J Healthc Risk Manag*. 2012;31(4):3-16.

- Herzer KR, Pronovost PJ. *Jt Comm J Qual Patient Saf*. 2015;41(11):522-528. Physician motivation: listening to what pay-for-performance programs and quality improvement collaboratives are telling us.

to feel that the newly envisioned field is where they need to be. For late adopters, it is important to emphasize how other like-minded individuals view the innovation. The focus should be on social norms rather than only the innovation's perceived benefits, innovators self-interest, or organizational hot topics. Such an approach ensures continuous focus on delivering the safest and highest possible quality patient care. As individuals embrace the dream, the status quo changes; eventually it becomes apparent which individuals will next need a more personalized invitation to join the early majority on the new field.

References:

1. Robinson L. A summary of diffusion of innovations. *Enabling Change.* January 2009:1-7 [online] http://www.enablingchange.com.au/Summary_Diffusion_Theory.pdf Accessed October 5, 2015.

2. Berwick DM. Disseminating innovations in health care. *JAMA.* 2003;289(15):1969-1975.

3. Rogers EM. *Diffusion of Innovations,* 5th ed. New York, NY: Free Press; 2003.

4. Greenhalgh T, Glenn R, Macfarlane F, Bate P, Kyriakidou O. Diffusion of innovations in service organizations: systemic review and recommendations. *Milbank Q.* 2004;82(4):581-629.

5. Moore GA. *Crossing Chasm: Marketing and Selling High-Tech Products to Mainstream Customers, Revised editions.* New York, NY: HarperCollins; 1999.

6. When, where and why did Winston Churchill say, "Never let a good crisis go to waste?" [website] https://www.quora.com/When-where-and-why-did-Winston-Churchill-say-%E2%80%9CNever-let-a-good-crisis-go-to-waste-%E2%80%9D. Accessed October 12, 2015.

7. Williams I. Organizational readiness for innovation in health care: some lessons from recent literature. *Health Serv Manage Res.* 2011;24(4):213-218.

8. Persaud DD. Enhancing Learning, Innovation, Adaptation and Sustainability in health care organizations. The ELIAS performance management framework. *Health Care Manager.* 2014;33(3):183-204.

9. Kotter JP. Leading change: why transformation efforts fail. *Harv Bus Rev.* 1995;73(2):59- 67.

10. Conway J. Getting boards on board: engaging governing boards in quality and safety. *Jt Comm J Qual Patient Saf.* 2008;34(4):214-220.

11. Cain M, Mittman R. *Diffusion of Innovation in Health Care.* Oakland CA; Institute for the Future, California Health Foundation; May 2002. [online] http://faculty.mercer.edu/thomas_bm/classes/641/Diffusion of Innovations in Healthcare.pdf Accessed October 5, 2015.

12. Bandura A. *Self-efficacy: The Exercise of Control.* New York, NY: WH Freeman; 1997.

13. Dixon RE. Centers for Disease Control and Prevention (CDC). Control of health-care-associated infections, 1961-2011. *MMWR Surveill Summ.* 2011;60(Suppl 4):58-63.

"THE DIFFICULTY LIES, NOT
IN THE NEW IDEAS, BUT IN
ESCAPING FROM THE OLD ONES."

– JM Keynes, *The General Theory of
Employment, Interest, and Money*

CHAPTER 10

SUSTAIN THE DREAM BY ECOSYSTEM COMMITMENT

John Littig, Gisele Norris

Once a vision is realized, *embraced, and implemented, the challenge becomes keeping the dream alive. The players are on the new field designed to ease their pain—there's no going back. This chapter provides insight on sustaining newly implemented practices and philosophies. In addition, it explores how to design innovation to respond to the internal and external influences that continuously affect the healthcare industry. Initiating and committing to a new direction is just the beginning. It is important to make adjustments that matter, to measure and communicate, to test and adjust, and, most importantly, to continually evolve. This is what will sustain the dream.*

WHEN GOING BACK ISN'T AN OPTION

In the film *Field of Dreams*, once Ray's ballfield was built, its beauty and belonging became undeniable. Foundational changes in risk management work the same way: once the new way is experienced and understood by the individuals that embrace it, going back just isn't an option. Shifts in core processes and professional mindsets must be accompanied by a sustainable implementation model that will enable the organization to pivot in response to external influences and internal modifications.

What will the next field look like? Is it difficult to imagine closely held Accountable Care Organizations (ACOs) incorporating significant bonuses or premium reductions to its members if they wear an advanced medical sensor? What if the ACO were collecting baseline values to identify slight shifts in health status indicators before they caused disease? While this future is exciting it's also a bit scary—collecting the right data, from the right person, with their consent; appropriate storage and deletion of data; the possibility of making an error in judgment; or information that can have an impact on many patients rather than one, and so on, are just a few of the foreseeable challenges now.

In addition to regulation and technology, payment models will continue to be modified. No matter how the Affordable Care Act (ACA) ultimately evolves, it is certain that the United States will need to continue to address the long-term cost curve of healthcare. The shift to paying for quality over quantity will advance aggressively. Direct contracts between employers and ACOs are likely. Price transparency and comparison will continue. Aggregation of hospitals and physicians groups across the entire spectrum of care, including post-acute and wellness, will persist. Corporate practice of medicine, the medical malpractice system, healthcare premium tax deductions, the diagnosis-related group (DRG) code system, palliative care, home healthcare delivery practices, may all survive in their current forms, others may evolve and some may become extinct—relics of a too expensive, mediocre system.

All change creates risk, and although the precise shape and form of that risk is unknowable, a principal role of the risk manager is to predict potential hazards and consequences and prepare the organization to master that risk. It is an is an intervention that truly takes root in an organization. When achieved, sustainable change helps an organization move from making conscious 'efforts to change' to establishing a new, accepted 'way of doing business.' Furthermore, sustainable change can feed on itself thus creating the continuous improvements most have given up on as an academic dream."[2(np)]

DESIGN TO EVOLVE AND LAST

Building the dream is the first step; sustaining the dream means facing a different set of challenges and requires consistent flexibility and innovation. Every dream evolves within constantly shifting internal and external environments. This evolution is especially true in today's consolidating healthcare industry where the culture of the healthcare system must adjust to new ownership, leadership, and application of organizational theory. As Peter Drucker famously cautioned, there is greater risk in approaching rapid change in turbulent times with outdated logic than in the very change itself.[3]

exciting and challenging role, and one that is instrumental in achieving organizational progress. As the journalist and humorist Robert Quillen once said, "Progress always involves risks. You can't steal second base and keep your foot on first."[1(p4)]

One of the greatest challenges to a new way of managing risk in healthcare will be to create meaningful systemic change that is sufficiently flexible to sustain the initial turbulent roll out and beyond. The ACA will unfold over a period of eight years. The ensuing regulations will require the implementation of many new systems and processes over the course of its roll out. Too often, changes that emerge in response to regulation are reactive and disjointed. In contrast, as business management consultant William Valutis opines on sustainable change, "Sustainable change

In addition to ensuring that the dream is relevant and updated, making room for continual modification also provides an opportunity to engage new participants and re-engage the original champions of the dream. By encouraging stakeholders to contribute

to the improvement and advancement of a goal, old ideas are made new again, stakeholders are re-energized, and original principles are communicated in fresh ways.

The Risk Authority Stanford leans on four fundamental principles to nurture new systems and processes:

- **MAKE CHANGE MATTER**
- **MEASURE AND COMMUNICATE IMPACT**
- **TEST AND ADJUST**
- **CONTINUALLY INNOVATE.**

Make Change Matter

In order to sustain the commitment to new systems and processes, staff must feel that new techniques will truly make a difference. In fact, research by social scientists shows that personal motivation to embrace an idea comes from sources external to their work environment and identifying and targeting those influences can help align an individual with the proposed organizational change.[4] Of course, identifying a shared and noble purpose is less of a challenge in the healthcare industry than it is in other business sectors. Most healthcare professionals have both a professional and personal interest in improving the quality of patient care.

The Risk Authority Stanford capitalizes on faculty physicians' commitment to improving patient care by creating physician risk management alliances. These alliances are a forum that fosters robust discussion and enables these physician leaders to identify risk management issues, engage in problem solving, and provide critical feedback to TRA Stanford and—more importantly—to their peers. Physicians view these forums, not as a risk management exercise, but as a way to improve their personal practice of medicine. As a result, many of these physicians become champions for risk management on the hospital floor. Their every day, peer-to-peer focus on patient safety, quality, and risk management principles influences the culture and practice of the medical staff. It motivates far more relevant and effective behavioral change than would a traditional continuing education course required by the CEO. As stated in a *strategy+business* article about change, "People need to be encouraged and motivated to change their behavior by those around them as much as they need incentives from the top."[5(np)]

Measure and Communicate Impact

As the shepherd of the dream outlined in this text, risk management's goal is to instill its principles within the enterprise by strengthening organizational philosophy and culture. But how does risk management know that it has been successful in implementing change? Perhaps more importantly, how does leadership know that their investments

Table 10.1: **The Risk Authority Stanford Strategies and Performance Measures**			
Strategy	**Metric**	**Governance**	**Continuous Improvement**
PEARL: Process for Early Assessment, Resolution and Learning	Frequency and severity.	Annual captive board discussion.	PEARL v2 is PEARL Care which includes proactive payment of patient medical bills.
DARTS: Decision Analysis Reserve and Trial Strategy	Loss development factors.	DARTS is used on a monthly basis, annual captive board discussion.	DARTS v2 includes a review of expert probabilities, inclusion of defense costs, and codification of best practices.
VDERM: Value Driven Enterprise Risk Management	VDERM is applied to all TRA Stanford business decisions, Net present value.	TRA Stanford leadership, board oversight.	VDERM is applied to all TRA Stanford business decisions, suggested for use in new areas and to assess problems of different sizes.

Table 10.1 shows the strategies TRA Stanford uses, along with the relevant metric used to measure their performance, what governance is in place and what continuous improvement is in store for that strategy.

have borne fruit? Identifying credible metrics to calculate effectiveness is critical to continued buy-in at all levels of the organization. The metrics themselves need not be novel mathematical formulas and in fact, in the data-rich healthcare environment, relevant metrics may already exist.

Like every element of risk management systems, metrics must be continually revisited, updated, and improved. But, practitioners can't lose sight of the basics, such as audits and check-ins. A simple, thoughtful measurement strategy can be elegant and enduring. The goal is to incorporate and sustain new standard operating procedures and incorporate them into the organizational DNA. Once the field is built, risk management can't go back. The new way will become *the* way and contributors will act accordingly.

Once the effectiveness of a proposed program or project has been measured, it must be communicated honestly to stakeholders at every level. Nurses, physicians and executives bring different perspectives and objectives to decision making and as such information should be provided in a way that is most suitable to each. Of course presenting data is only half the challenge. The story that the metrics tell must ultimately be communicated. Dashboard graphics are informative, but weaving an anecdote around those graphics multiplies their influence. Regardless of the nature of the presentation, every level of communication must instill trust, transparency, and authenticity. Honest reporting of failures as well as victories furthers process improvement and sets the tone for staff and clinicians at every level to admit weaknesses and point out opportunities for enhancement.

 Frequent and effective communication with the C-suite is especially important in the current environment of rapidly changing healthcare leadership. Early adopters are apt to occupy those positions. To maintain relevance, risk managers must establish champions among multiple executives and have a story ready for incoming leadership. While the success of Ray's ballfield in *Field of*

 Dreams was self-evident, the success of a healthcare risk management program is more subtle. This is where the selected tactics such as decision analysis and design thinking (see chapter 8 of this book) are important. Using the traditional metrics for risk management successes, losses, and premiums may not tell the story of risk management transformation.

Test and Adjust

Testing and tweaking should happen at several points in the process. One way to gain employee buy-in is to apply quantitative and qualitative methods to simulate processes from start to finish, prior to implementing any change. The Risk Authority Stanford has found that participants are more inclined to adopt new techniques when they understand their role and the expected influence of their actions. The approach not only quells employee fears about what comes next, but also provides a forum for questions, inputs, and tweaks. When a nurse manager is concerned about the consequence a given change will have on his or her staff, practical and effective use of a VDERM process allows the team to take concerns into account as part of the analysis. As a result, staff understand not only the change that is expected of them, but how they might confront perceived challenges and the importance of their personal contribution.

A robust program is built to sustain stressors. The unexpected will happen and risk management will need a ready answer. The key is having a toolkit prepared so that these events are proof points rather than stumbling blocks for the new way.

Conducting periodic tabletop exercises to help think through risk scenarios can be helpful in understanding roles, responsibilities, and processes in the event of risk. TRA Stanford built a tabletop simulation exercise around an established apology and disclosure process. The exercise revealed the best words and phrases to use when communicating to a patient about an unanticipated medical outcome. Actors carried out role plays as patient family members and staff physicians. Frontline risk managers and claims staff observed and recorded the interactions, and rated various physician responses to identify the words that resulted in the most positive interactions. The output from this simulation helps the risk management department provide consultation and guidance to physicians engaged in actual apology and disclosure conversations.

As discussed in chapter 4, in situ simulation improves care delivery systems through the reenactment of challenging patient care situations. This allows teams to explore and correct operational and

| Honest reporting of failures as well as victories furthers process improvement.

system breakdowns.[6] These scenarios can include the same team involved in the real situation and provide them an opportunity to relive the moment and determine how an issue might have been avoided. Such simulations are non-punitive in nature and typically provide the team with a sense of closure and positive learning, team-building experiences. Whenever possible, feedback and conclusions garnered during such simulations are used to inform and adapt systems and processes.

Continually Innovate

It has long been said that change is the only constant. Right now is a time of unprecedented possibilities for human health. Bioinformatics, genomics, and other emerging disciplines promise to transform the very concept of medicine—from treating disease after it has struck to predicting it, preventing it, and promoting lifelong health. In this dynamic new millennium, healthcare systems must choose to innovate or stagnate. The choice to innovate is not a one-time pledge, but a daily commitment to progress. Luckily, healthcare institutions are replete with very smart people, many of whom have great ideas. The Stanford University Medical Network capitalizes on local brainpower to continually think anew to improve healthcare and encourage cross-pollination of ideas within and beyond the walls of its medical center.

It is in this environment that The Risk Authority Stanford maintains inventive efforts to sustain the dream of a new and improved field—one that respects beneficial tradition at its core, is undeterred by the challenge of rapid change, and does not rely on yesterday's logic. This is the way forward to generate evidence-based practices and effectively redesign risk and safety ecosystems as inspired by TRA Stanford's north star—patients.

References

1. Quillen R. Corks and curls. *Spartanburg (SC) Herald*, August 11, 1927:p4,col5. [online] https://news.google.com/newspapers?id=EjcsAAAAIBAJ&sjid=W8oEAAAAIBAJ&pg=7125,4044835&dq=can-t-steal-second+foot-on-first&hl=en. Accessed October 5, 2015.

2. Valutis W. Sustainable change: making it happen: the secrets to creating sustainable change. *Simplicity HR*. [online] http://www.simplicityhr.com/sustainable-change. Accessed October 5, 2015.

3. Drucker P. *Managing in Turbulent Times*. New York, NY: Harper Paperbacks; 1980.

4. Aiken C, Galper D, Keller S. Winning hearts and minds: the secrets of sustaining change. In: Jenkins A, ed. *Lean Management New Frontiers for Financial Institutions*. New York, NY:McKinsey and Company; 2011:46-53. [online] http://www.mckinsey.com/global_locations/pacific/australia/en/latest_thinking/~/media/3d980de89d5d4c91b3d01793afe03c3b.ashx. Accessed October 5, 2015.

5. Harshak A, Aguirre D, Brown A. Making change happen and making it stick. *strategy+ business*. December 20, 2010. [online] http://www.strategy-business.com/article/00057?pg=all. Accessed October 5, 2015.

6. Braddock CH III, Szaflarski N, Forsey L, Abel L, Hernandez-Boussard T, Morton J. The TRANSFORM patient safety project: a microsystem approach to improving outcomes on inpatient units. *J Gen Intern Med*. 2015;30(4):425-433.

"WHAT YOU GET BY ACHIEVING
YOUR GOALS IS NOT AS
IMPORTANT AS WHAT YOU BECOME
BY ACHIEVING YOUR GOALS."

– Henry David Thoreau

CORN, CATCH, AND CARS: COMMITTING TO A FRESH FUTURE

James Conway

TWILIGHT AND TURBULENCE COMBINE TO FOSTER SUCCESS

Once an innovation has achieved initial success, efforts cannot be allowed to go dormant at the twilight. Those at the transformational leading edge of enterprise risk management (ERM) innovation exude excitement and affirmation for those colleagues, both personally and professionally, working around and with them. Embracing this new model challenges the current state with an approach anchored in vision, values, and outcomes while being supported by learning, improvement, structure, and process. The ERM concept discussed herein is comprehensive. It calls for a process that includes: risk identification, assessment, evaluation, mitigation plus value-creation with iterative opportunity to monitor and react as indicated—across the enterprise.[1]

ERM sets the stage for key leadership partnerships to be created across the spectrum of healthcare from trustees and executives to clinicians, patients, and family members. With this new framework and these partnerships, challenges become opportunities for change. There is vast potential for improvement of clinical, financial, service, and experience outcomes for patients, family members, staff, and communities. Respect for the process and the shared successes flourishes.

Accountability for managing risk is shared. These outcomes are why values-based leaders entered healthcare and risk management. Reenergized, after seeing so much potential, and drawing great courage from encountering a community of like-minded people, attention must be turned back to the farm and the corn.

Overwhelming, daunting, and impossible are but a few words describing the healthcare scene today as reform of seemingly everything takes hold.

> **This twilight should be embraced as a time for new thought, rather than a time for repose.**

Executives, managers, and staff alike find comfort in equating the current landscape to drowning under a waterfall of unconnected initiatives. Turbulent. There is an infection of "projectitis," so to speak, and unsustained change and improvement. It is as it would have been had Ray, in *Field of Dreams*, not gone the distance, not taken the journey to Doc Graham, not lit the ballfield, or walked away and not played catch on the new field with his father. Leaders in these ranks recognize that there are considerable risks, tremendous waste, and extensive harm with practices that do not respect all: the patient, family, staff, organization, and community. Dramatic change is needed.

This twilight should be embraced as a time for new thought, rather than a time for repose.

There is a realization that the more things change, the more they stay the same, but at this juncture, the sky looks different. Change is hard, takes great effort, and the transition strategies are unclear. These days, resources are scarce. Results at an organization may already be consistent or better than overall industry results, so why bother to try to change? If an organization has laggards at the helm, is the argument from the ranks to mow down the entire field the first strategy to present? Traditional risk management practice—the corn—while not perfect, may be doing a good job and modest incremental implementation of new approaches may just be the best use of organizational time, attention, and resources. However, this approach to risk management appears to be struggling to show its value.[2,3] This may not seem like the time for chancy business efforts. Staff is burned out. Patients and their families are evolving into healthcare consumers with options and stronger opinions about their care experiences and outcomes. Innovation is great but also an added expense. Many organizations don't have the resources to spare to consider the distance, let alone "Go The Distance."

What's wrong with waiting a while and just being part of the late majority?

Terence Mann, in *Field of Dreams*, comes to see enormous possibility arising from partnering with Ray but, for others, maybe innovation and transformative change seem too disruptive to be considered opportunities. The question

> **The question must be asked: What should be invented for new ideas to get lift, add value, and be sustained?**

as to whether it will make a difference resonates around both the board table and the water cooler. There are multiple examples of tremendous interest in, and awareness of, the need for the elements of change.[4] Everyone attends the lecture, reads the book, tweets the phrase, and quotes the speaker. Neither individual nor organizational behaviors are changing materially to ease the pain of dysfunction. For leaders, the course ahead sounds daunting. The question must be asked: What should be invented for new ideas to get lift, add value, and be sustained?

MOVING AHEAD AND A LITTLE DEEPER

All healthcare must continually evolve its service to the mission of benefitting patients, family members, and communities. *Field of Dreams* demonstrates the exceptional power of the visionary leader partnering with the early adopter to take a new course. While acknowledging their essential role in any successful change initiative, in complex systems like the application of ERM in healthcare, success takes dramatically more: consideration of others, respect for the system, sensitivity to the needs of the future. Otherwise, passion-driven delivery of an innovative idea will ultimately fail. It will be built, but others will not act to sustain the vision.

For enterprise risk management to be positioned for success it must embrace the true notion of enterprise as a system- or organization-wide approach and not just the work of risk, compliance, finance, or some other individual or department-based initiative. Risk management must be out and about, an essential partner, contributing to overall success in all areas, and specifically, quality, safety, and compliance. As the Institute for Healthcare Improvement (IHI) has taught in the *Framework for Leadership Improvement* when department heads and clinicians ask "what's in it for me?", aim/vision statements for enterprise risk management must make clear what is trying to be accomplished collectively as well as individually.[5] Everyone must be able to see their role and place, their improved state, and their benefits.

There must be active engagement of leaders and nurturing of new leaders at every level, including frontline staff, patients, family members, governance and executive management throughout the process. The enterprise risk management system must be positioned to show its value toward achieving balanced clinical,

Everyone must be able to see their role and place, their improved state, and their benefits.

financial, service, and experience outcomes. In the new order of healthcare reform it is clear that, over time, organizations with the best integrated measurable outcomes will win. For the enterprise risk management system to be part of the Institute of Medicine (IOM)-defined learning healthcare system, its success will be dependent on and driven by science and informatics, patient clinician partnerships, aligned incentives, and culture.[6]

This work will require a model for change that is lived, breathed, and applied relentlessly. John Kotter, a leading expert in change, has taught that transformational change requires that all of the following be considered:

- Change needs to happen quickly and with passion.
- Leadership and guidance work together not only in risk management but across the organization.

- The vision for the work is understood by all and shared widely.
- Authorize and encourage staff to act on the vision.
- Incorporate small successes into the program and celebrate them.
- Fold advances into projects to seed enhancements and consolidate improvements to produce more change.
- Build the changes into the way the organization works.[7]

Implementing enterprise risk management will require each and every step, not only by the visionary leaders and early adopters, but also by growing numbers of members of the organizational community. Each must come to the field and contribute to the vision and share the learnings broadly when they return to their own space, community, family—and the corn.

WHAT VOICE WILL BE HEARD?

Ultimately, the secret of quality is love. You have to love your patient, you have to love your profession, you have to love your God. If you have love, you can then work backward to monitor and improve the system.

   – Avedis Donabedian,
      2001 interview with F. Mullan

As leaders settle into the routines of change, armed with recommended and evidence-based strategies and tactics, they will recognize that time and attention must be given to The Voice. A sense of urgency will arise to the value of engaging the hearts, as well as the minds, of all managers of risk to seek a better way.[8] Healthcare's own Shoeless Joe, Ray, Terence, Annie, Karin—and even naysayers like Mark—help to raise, debate, and ask hard questions to keep the resolve of leaders focused on what is *good*. The whole plethora of experts—armed with their stories and their experiences—must commit to working together to sustain radical change toward managing risks in healthcare. Uncompromising and incessant, the focus on the patient, their safety, the health of the organization and the individuals who work there—is the goal. To be successful, the culture in place must make this the mantra of daily work.

WHAT DISRUPTION WILL EARLY ADOPTERS BRING TO THE FIELD?

The early adopter can bring lessons from immersion in the status quo to the table to make change. As embodied by the character Terence Mann in the *Field of Dreams* metaphor, he'll enter the corn armed with the tough questions.[9] Terence will have firsthand knowledge of the complexity of what he seeks to disrupt. His return launches the sense of urgency for change. His insights and the force of his leadership will anchor his ideas to establish creative tension by showing not only the direction of the overall vision but by illuminating the reality of current practice.[10] With this transparency and mindfulness to what is, profound gaps in managing risk and the urgency needed to radicalize work toward improvement

> **Despite the challenges and the recognition that many change efforts fail, they know that as the sun sets and the light dims, the right thing to do will be to look up.**

will be realized. The need to capitalize on which risks to take to generate action will also be clarified. The tension that arises from his return will drive respectful dialogue, change, and ultimately progress.

What will twilight bring?

Ray is rebuilding relationships and strengthening existing ones. He is also now responsible for the field—no turning back—and builds a sense of urgency to establish the value and contribution his innovation will bring to the community.

Those around him do more than benefit from his vision and purpose. They appear and rally to share it. They partner with others to nullify the potential slide backward toward failure. They keep on the path toward change they believe in. They come to the field in their cars from far and wide—basking in how it reminds them of why they got into healthcare in the first place. As clinicians, administrators, risk managers, or patients—the seats are there— inviting them to sit down, to observe, to participate. They have gathered to engage in the disruption of convention to create a mindset devoted to improvement—to regain something good. Despite the challenges and the recognition that many change efforts fail, they know that as the sun sets and the light dims, the right thing to do will be to look up.

References

1. Driver J, Bernard R. Enterprise risk management and its relationship to the Wizard of Oz. *Resources Magazine.* Summer 2013;37-39.

2. ECRI Institute. Strategies to prove risk management = value. *Risk Manage Rep.* 2011;30(3):1,4-9.

3. Widemer L. Is risk management obsolete? *Risk Management.* April 2013. [online] http://www.rmmagazine.com/2013/04/12/is-risk-management-obsolete/. Accessed October 5, 2015.

4. Conway J, Federico F, Stewart K, Campbell MJ. *Respectful Management of Serious Clinical Adverse Events.* 2nd ed. Cambridge, MA: Institute for Healthcare Improvement; 2011. [online] http://www.ihi.org/resources/pages/ihiwhitepapers/respectfulmanagementseriousclinicalaeswhitepaper.aspx Accessed October 4, 2015.

5. Provost L, Miller D, Reinertsen J. *IHI Framework for Leadership for Improvement.* Cambridge, MA: Institute for Healthcare Improvement; February 2006. [online] http://www.ihi.org/resources/Pages/Tools/IHIFrameworkforLeadershipforImprovement.aspx. Accessed October 5, 2015.

6. Smith M, Saunders R, Stuckhardt L, McGinnis JM, eds. *Best Care at Lower Cost: the Path to Continuously Learning Health Care in America.* Washington, DC: National Academies Press; 2013.

7. Kotter JP. Leading change: why transformation efforts fail. *Harv Bus Rev.* 1995;73(2):59-67.

8. Kotter JP, Cohen DS. *The Heart of Change: Real-life Stories of How People Change Their Organizations.* Boston, MA: Harvard Business Press; 2002.

9. Laskowski N. The disruptor's secret: question everything. Techtarget. November 2014. [online] http://searchcio.techtarget.com/opinion/The-disruptors-secret-Question-everything. Accessed October 5, 2015.

10. Senge PM. The leader's new work: building learning organizations. *Sloan Manage Rev.* 1990;32(1):7-23.

WHAT WILL YOU BUILD…

WHAT PAIN WILL YOU EASE...

HOW WILL YOU GO THE DISTANCE…

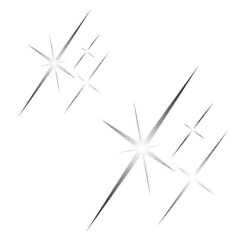

PLOT OUTLINE FOR THE UNIVERSAL PICTURES FILM *FIELD OF DREAMS*

 Setting: **Dyersville, Iowa**
Time: **Mid-'80s**
Opening: **A Dream Begins**

While walking his Iowa corn field at twilight, idealistic farmer Ray Kinsella hears a voice that only he can hear. The Voice suggests direction for Ray's life in abstract terms to set the plot in motion with three directives: "If You Build It, He Will Come," "Ease His Pain," and "Go The Distance." Each serves to shape a phase in Ray's pursuit of answers that he believes will take him, his family and his friends to a better place.

If You Build It, He Will Come

- The first phase of Ray's journey involves the building of a ballfield in the middle of his farm.

- Ray and his wife Annie—while aware of the risk of Ray's dream—move forward. Both she and their daughter Karin help to establish the innovation.

- Ray mows down a portion of his corn crop to build a field he believes will create a place for the discredited 1919 Chicago "Black Sox" baseball star Shoeless Joe Jackson to play ball again.

- Unaware of Ray's intention for building the field—his community scoffs and sees him as "crazy" as they watch him make this unexplainable change to his farm.

- Time passes and Ray waits for confirmation that his field will realize his goal.

- Ray, Annie and Karin recognize the value of the innovation when Shoeless Joe first appears, meets them, and plays ball revisiting his love of the game.
- Once Shoeless Joe (an early majority) meets Ray and trusts his innovation, Joe invites other players from the 1919 team to join him. He leaves each night by disappearing into the remaining field of corn.
- Ray has finished the first step but has yet to complete work toward his dream.

Ease His Pain

- Time again passes—The Voice presents another challenge to Ray to create yet another opportunity to affect the happiness of an individual.
- Shoeless Joe has returned with his teammates and they have taken the field. Ray is not clear on his next step but feels there is something more to his mission than to bring back the 1919 Black Sox.
- Annie emerges as a leader in her community by supporting and providing access to ideas that challenge the status quo at a community meeting where the writings of Terence Mann—a character based on JD Salinger—are being considered to be banned from schools. She makes explicit that a lack of shared understanding from the past can be a barrier to the future.
- As Annie initiates a debate on the value of being open to other perspectives, Ray realizes that Terence Mann—and

addressing his pain and frustration—is the key to moving forward. Ray does research to confirm his course of action before he proceeds.

- Ray drives from Iowa to Boston to meet the influential writer, introduce him to his innovation and invite him to participate in piecing together the next step of the puzzle The Voice has presented him with.
- Ray cajoles Terence to join him at a Boston Red Sox baseball game, convinced his presence will ease the pain of the writer and Ray's discomfort due to the lack of clarity of the future of his actions. While at the game, Ray and Terence create a bond when the next step toward resolving The Voice's direction appears to both men. Terence then joins Ray voluntarily as a like-minded partner to be an early adopter and lend credibility to the project in the face of uncertainty.

Go The Distance

- The third part of the journey recognizes the value in tradition and love of baseball.
- Terence and Ray continue on their trip to enable another individual to realize a dream.
- Having taken direction from The Voice at the Boston ballpark, they travel to Minnesota to meet Archibald "Moonlight" Doc Graham, another man with a dream of baseball, who chose another destiny as a physician.

- Doc Graham's story is introduced to Ray and Terence through stories from his community about the doctor who has passed away.
- Ray and Terence decide to leave town to head to Iowa when Ray, walking the streets of Doc's town, encounters his ghost.
- The older Graham speaks wistfully of his dream of baseball and his recognition that his role in life was to be a husband and doctor.
- Seeing no direction from the experience, they return to Iowa only to meet on the road the young Moonlight Graham as an idealistic young athlete with a dream of playing ball.
- Upon arriving to the field, the young Graham is welcomed into the dream— and sets his sights on playing ball as a teammate with the players now present on the field.

Closing: Resolving the Dream

- Despite the success the primary characters see in the field, there are outsiders that have concerns.
- The lack of ability to recognize the dream is represented by Annie's brother Mark who as a protagonist continues to advocate that Ray and Annie sell the farm—as its value has been lost due to the building of the ballfield.

- In light of this challenge, Ray considers the perceptions of those around him. His daughter Karin states her belief that the field will be of value to others. Terrance finds inspiration in her insight to poetically articulate in no uncertain terms that the field will be a success as it represents what is *good*.
- As the argument ensues, Mark in frustration has an accident in which Karin becomes injured.
- Moonlight Graham—responding to his calling to be a doctor—leaves his dream behind to emerge from the field and see to Karin's condition. His action nullifies two risks: Karin is treated and Mark becomes aware of the dream.
- Mark sees the full team on the field, sees the value of Ray's actions, and becomes supportive.
- Terence explores his dreams by joining the team as they return to "the corn."
- As the sun sets, Ray again sees opportunity as his father—a former baseball player who didn't succeed in the sport which damaged their relationship—has appeared. They meet and play catch as cars arrive to ensure the future of the field as a beacon to what is good for their community, for the players, for Terence and for Ray, his family and the farm.

APPENDIX TWO

EPIGRAPH CITATIONS

Every effort was made to confirm the original source for the epigraphs used throughout the text.
— the editors

Prologue:
Shaw GB. *Back to Methuselah, act I, Selected Plays with Prefaces*, vol. 2. New York, NY: Dodd, Meade; 1949[pg7].

Voltaire: Letter to Frederick William, Prince of Prussia (28 November 1770). In: Tallentyre, SG, ed. *Voltaire in His Letters Being a Selection from His Correspondence*. New York, NY: GP Putnam's Sons; 1919[pg232].

Gawande A. Failure and Rescue. *The New Yorker News Desk*. June 2, 2012. http://www.newyorker.com/news/news-desk/failure-and-rescue. Accessed October 8, 2015.

Chapter 1:
Einstein A. *Einstein on Cosmic Religion and Other Opinions and Aphorisms*. Mineola, NY: Dover Publications, Inc; 2009[pg97].

Chapter 2:
Kennedy JF. Address in the Assembly Hall at the Paulskirche in Frankfurt, West Germany, June 25, 1963. Online by Gerhard Peters and John T. Woolley, *The American Presidency Project*. http://www.presidency.ucsb.edu/ws/?pid=9303. Accessed October 8, 2015.

Chapter 3:
Thoreau, HD. *Walden 150th Anniversary Edition*. Princeton, NJ: Princeton University Press; 2004[pg324].

Chapter 4:
Eisenhower, DW. Address at Bradley University, Peoria, Illinois, September 25, 1956. http://www.eisenhower.archives.gov/all_about_ike/quotes.html. Accessed October 8, 2015.

Chapter 5:
Levitt T. *Marketing Imagination: New Expanded Edition*. New York, NY: The Free Press; 1986[pgxxii].

Chapter 6:

Jobs S. 'You've got to find what you love,' Jobs says. *Stanford Report*, published June 14, 2005. http://news.stanford.edu/news/2005/june15/jobs-061505.html. Accessed November 18, 2015.

Ben Franklin quote: https://www.quora.com/Where-and-when-did-Benjamin-Franklin-say-Tell-me-and-I-forget-teach-me-and-I-may-remember-involve-me-and-I-learn. Accessed November 18, 2015.

Chapter 7:

Moore, C. *Daniel H. Burnham, Architect, Planner of Cities, volume 2, chapter XXV*. Boston, MA: Houghton Mifflin; 1921[pg147].

Chapter 8:

Berwick DM. *Escape Fire: Lessons for the Future of Health Care*. New York, NY: The Commonwealth Fund; 2002(pg55). http://www.commonwealthfund.org/usr_doc/berwick_escapefire_563.pdf. Accessed November 18, 2015.

Chapter 9:

The person who says it cannot be done should not interrupt the person doing it. Chinese Proverb http://quoteinvestigator.com/2015/01/26/doing/. Accessed November 18, 2015.

Chapter 10:

Keynes JM. *The General Theory of Employment, Interest and Money*. [1936]. Reproduced as E-book by: South Australia: The University of Adelaide Library; 2014[Preface]. https://ebooks.adelaide.edu.au/k/keynes/john_maynard/k44g/complete.html. Accessed November 18, 2015.

Epilogue:

Henry David Thoreau quote: http://www.goodreads.com/quotes/597758-what-you-get-by-achieving-your-goals-is-not-as. Accessed November 18, 2015.

Donabedian A. A founder of quality assessment encounters a troubled system firsthand. Interview by Fitzhugh Mullan. *Health Aff (Millwood)*. 2001;20(1):137-141[pg140].

INDEX

Bold numbers indicate illustrations.

medication delivery
  and ballfield (as metaphor), 112–115
microsystem approach, 68–69, 72
Mission Zero, 109–110
motivation, 23–32, 62, 77, 148
  of clinicians, 69–71
  of employees, 90
  and evidence, 24–26
  and inspiration, 26–28
  and intuition, 31–32
  and storytelling, 28–31

O
organizational culture, 39, 48–49, 65, 82, 94–95,
      142, 147–148. *See also* safety culture
organizational ecosystem, 48–56
  and ERM, 50–51
  of hospitals, 49
  and innovation, 12–15
  redesign, 51–53
organizational improvement, 12–13

P
partnerships, 6, 16–18, 51–53, 62–68, 77–78
  and time management, 122
passion, 31, 158
patient centeredness, 72, 76, 84, 97, 105, 150
  and TRA Stanford (The Risk Authority Stanford),
      76–84
patient perspective, 64–66, 105
patient safety and quality, 28–29, 113–115
patients
  and clinicians, 64–66
PEARL (Process for Early Assessment, Resolution
      and Learning), 30–31, 81–82, 149
perception, 138–142
performance measurement, 148–150
Peters, Tom, 49
physician champions, 148
PPACA (Patient Protection and Affordable Care
      Act), 41, 146–147
Pronovost, Peter, 9

R
relatability, 140
risk
  and farm (as metaphor), 26–28
risk domains, healthcare, **50**
risk management
  education, 95–97
  effectiveness, ix–x
  evolution of, 37–41, **93**
  structure, 51
Risk Management in Residency, 96–97
risk managers
  and clinicians, 70
Rogers Innovation Scale, **6**, 6–8, **14**, 37, 69

S
safe patient handling, 55–56
safety culture, 12, 48–49, 68, 108, 112
self insurance, 132–133
Semmelwis, Ignaz, 15
"Shoeless" Joe Jackson (character), 11, 16, 25,
      28, 122
silos, 42, 49, 62
simulation, 9, 82–83, 150–152
Six Sigma, 48
space, untraditional, 29
stakeholders, 147
  and medical error, 103–106
Stanford Committee for Professional Satisfaction
      and Support (SCPSS), 97
Stanford Operation System, 48–49
Stanford University Medical Network, 9, 30, 76
  Lucile Packard Children's Hospital, 139, 141
  Stanford Children's Health, 106–107
  Stanford Health Care, 68, 76
  Stanford Hospital, 54–55
storytelling, 28–30
  and motivation, 28–31
sustaining change, 145–152, 156–160
systems approach, 29

T
Taleb, Nassim, 120
TeamSTEPPS™, 68
teamwork, 42, 68–71, 105, 109–113, 151–152

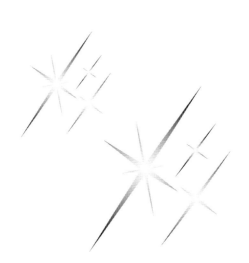